P9-CBA-121

THE COLD WAR

CHRONICLE OF AMERICA'S WARS

Josepha Sherman

🏛 LERNER PUBLICATIONS COMPANY

MINNEAPOLIS

Introduction: President John F. Kennedy *(far right, leaning forward)* and his advisers discuss U.S. strategy during the Cuban Missile Crisis, October 1962.

Chapter 1: U.S. and Soviet flags. The United States and the Soviet Union were the world's two most powerful nations during the second half of the twentieth century.

Chapter 2: A German family walks through the rubble of their destroyed city. World War II left much of Europe in ruins.

Chapter 3: Senator Joseph McCarthy of Wisconsin *(in foreground)* led the attacks against Communism in the 1950s. McCarthy's bullying style and reckless attacks would come to be known as McCarthyism.

Chapter 4: Communist officials from North Korea and China meet during the Korean War to discuss a possible cease-fire agreement in Kaesong, Korea, in 1953.

Chapter 5: Cuban leader Fidel Castro *(left)* and Nikita Khrushchev *(right)* were both political enemies of the United States. Cuba's geographic closeness to the United States made Castro a valuable ally to the Soviet Union.

Chapter 6: U.S. soldiers march through rice fields in Vietnam. The Vietnam War would become one of the most costly conflicts of the Cold War.

Chapter 7: Soviet leader Leonid Brezhnev *(left)* and U.S. president Richard M. Nixon *(right)* at a summit meeting. The policy of détente would bring some progress toward ending hostile relations between the United States and the Soviet Union.

Chapter 8: Soviet leader Mikhail Gorbachev *(left)* and U.S. president Ronald Reagan *(right)* exchange greetings at a summit meeting. The two leaders got along well and developed a strong relationship, which helped with their negotiations.

Copyright © 2004 by Josepha Sherman

All rights reserved. International copyright secured. No part of this book may be reproduced, stored in a retrieval system, or transmitted in any form or by any means—electronic, mechanical, photocopying, recording, or otherwise—without the prior written permission of Lerner Publications Company, except for the inclusion of brief quotations in an acknowledged review.

Lerner Publications Company
A division of Lerner Publishing Group
241 First Avenue North
Minneapolis, MN 55401

Website address: www.lernerbooks.com

Library of Congress Cataloging-in-Publication Data

Sherman, Josepha.
    The Cold War / by Josepha Sherman.
       p.   cm. — (Chronicle of America's wars)
    Summary: Chronicles the Cold War, from its origins in the Soviet Revolution as the twentieth century began to the collapse of the Soviet Union as the century closed.
    Includes bibliographical references and index.
    ISBN: 0–8225–0150–3 (lib. bdg. : alk. paper)
    1. Cold War—Juvenile literature. 2. Soviet Union—Foreign relations—1917–1945—Juvenile literature.
3. Soviet Union—Foreign relations—1945–1991—Juvenile literature. 4. World politics—1945–1989.
[1. Cold War. 2. Soviet Union—Foreign relations—United States. 3. United States—Foreign relations—Soviet Union.
4. World politics—1945–1989.] I. Title. II. Series.
D843.S454 2004
909.82'5—dc21   2002156559

Manufactured in the United States of America
1 2 3 4 5 6 – JR – 09 08 07 06 05 04

TABLE OF CONTENTS

INTRODUCTION

The year was 1962, and the world was on the brink of nuclear war. The world's two superpowers, the United States and the Union of Soviet Socialist Republics (USSR), were engaged in a tense showdown.

The two nations had been enemies for nearly 20 years, although they had never fought. Instead, their rivalry had come to be known as the "Cold War"—a kind of chilly standoff, instead of a "hot," or fighting, war.

For nearly 20 years, the two rivals had been engaged in a dangerous arms race. Each side worked feverishly to build more powerful weapons than the other. In the 1950s, both nations had developed hydrogen bombs. A single one of these nuclear weapons could wipe out an entire city in minutes. By the late 1950s, both superpowers had built enough bombs to destroy the earth several times over. Each nation had fleets of long-range bomber aircraft on constant airborne patrol, ready to strike at their rival at any time.

Yet in 1962, the United States held a crucial advantage in the arms race. It had nuclear missiles based in the nation of Turkey that could be launched from the United States to hit the USSR in minutes. The Soviets had no such bases close to the United States. But in April, the Soviets began to secretly install missiles on the island of Cuba, only 90 miles off the coast of Florida. With these missiles in place,

from the USSR. And a nuclear strike from the Soviet Union (as the USSR was often called) would surely mean a nuclear response from the United States.

A key element to nuclear strategy is deterrence—that is, knowing that a nuclear attack would lead to a counterattack. Destroying your enemy would lead to your own destruction. A phrase of the era, in fact, summed up the strategy of deterrence—Mutual Assured Destruction, or MAD, for short.

In the event of a nuclear war, the United States and the USSR were likely to attack with hundreds of nuclear weapons. Hundreds of millions of people would be killed. Cities would be reduced to charred rubble. Entire landscapes—animals, forests, vegetation, farms—would be wiped out. The millions of tons of dust and debris created by the explosions would be hurled into the air, creating a massive cloud that would block out the sun for months, perhaps years. This cloud and the earth beneath it would be contaminated by deadly poisonous radioactive fallout. In this scenario, called a "nuclear winter," it was a very real possibility that all life on earth would cease to exist.

the Soviets would have the ability to launch a quick nuclear strike on the United States.

In October a U.S. spy plane discovered the Cuban missile sites. U.S. president John F. Kennedy had some very difficult decisions to make. As a matter of national security, he could not allow the Soviets to build nuclear missiles so close to the United States. Yet sending U.S. aircraft and U.S. troops to Cuba to destroy the missile sites might trigger a nuclear attack from Soviet bomber aircraft and long-range missiles launched

As the Cuban Missile Crisis reached a climax in October 1962, President Kennedy and Soviet premier (leader) Nikita S. Khrushchev kept in constant communication. A peaceful settlement to the problem had to be reached. The fate of the world depended on it.

> EYEWITNESS QUOTE:
> THE CUBAN MISSLE CRISIS
>
> "Nuclear catastrophe was hanging by a thread . . . and we weren't counting days or hours, but minutes."
>
> —General Anatoly Gribkov, chief of operations, Soviet Army

THE RISE
1) OF THE SUPERPOWERS

In the 1900s, the United States and the Soviet Union were nations with very different methods of government. The two countries also had very different economic systems and histories.

THE UNITED STATES

Native Americans were the original inhabitants of the North American continent. These peoples lived in numerous groups throughout North America. In the late 1400s, explorers from Europe began creating settlements in what they called the New World. The largest European settlements in the area that later became the United States were along the Atlantic coast of North America. White settlers from Great Britain began arriving there in the early 1600s. Many of the Native Americans were pushed aside as these settlements, or colonies, grew throughout the 1600s and into the 1700s. By the mid-1700s, Great Britain governed all of the American colonies.

Under Great Britain's loose colonial rule, many white male American citizens developed a tradition of freedom and democracy. Generally speaking, most American males who owned property had the right to vote for people to represent them in government. But Native Americans, African Americans, and women did not always enjoy these rights.

In 1775 disputes with Britain led many Americans to revolt against British rule.

This marked the beginning of the American Revolution (or Revolutionary War). A year later, in July 1776, the new American government declared its independence from Great Britain. It did so by creating and adopting the Declaration of Independence. This document declared that "all men are created equal" and have the right to "Life, Liberty, and the Pursuit of Happiness." The new nation, the United States of America, fought a long and bloody war against the British to secure its independence. This war officially ended in 1783.

In the 1800s, the United States experienced spectacular growth. American settlers moved westward across the continent, claiming or purchasing new land. The United States grew to cover much of North America. By the middle of the 1900s, the United States had become the richest nation on earth.

Yet despite the Declaration of Independence, Native Americans, African American slaves, and women did not have equal rights. Native Americans were pushed off land they had lived on for hundreds, sometimes thousands, of years. When they fought to keep their land, these natives were often slaughtered by U.S. troops.

During the early decades of the United States, most African Americans were slaves with no personal freedom. These men, women, and children worked for their entire lives for little or no pay. Their owners had the right to sell, beat, or kill them. Slavery was not outlawed in the United States until the 1860s. Since then, African Americans have had to fight long and hard to gain equal rights.

Early in U.S. history, women enjoyed few legal rights. In most states, they were

American citizens rose up to fight against their British rulers during the American Revolution.

considered the property of their husbands. Women were not allowed to vote in national elections until 1920. In modern times, women still struggle to be treated as equals in American society.

DEMOCRACY AND CAPITALISM IN THE UNITED STATES

The U.S. system of government is democratic. In democratic elections, citizens vote for people to represent them in local, state, and national governments. In turn, these representatives are expected to make and enforce laws that work for the best interests of the people they represent. Elected officials are often members of political parties, which represent the beliefs and priorities of particular voters. Throughout the 1900s, two major parties dominated the U.S. political scene—the Democratic Party and the Republican Party. Citizens often voted for the candidates of the party that best fit their values.

The United States' system of laws, the Constitution and the Bill of Rights, guarantees the right of free speech for all citizens. By law, Americans have the right to think, write, and say what they want—no matter how unpopular it might be—without fear of imprisonment. This includes the right to criticize and question the government and its actions. This freedom of speech, combined with the democratic voting process, means that U.S. leaders must listen to their citizens if they wish to remain in power. Leaders who go against the will of the people run the risk of being voted out of office.

Freedom is also a key element of the American economic system. The United

The First Amendment

The First Amendment of the U.S. Bill of Rights states that, "Congress shall make no law respecting an establishment of religion, or prohibiting the free exercise thereof; or abridging the freedom of speech, or of the press; or the right of the people peaceably to assemble, and to petition the Government for a redress of grievances."

In other words, the First Amendment says that Americans have the right to say and believe what they choose without fear of the government punishing them. The amendment also states that Americans have the right to complain to the government ("to petition the Government for a redress of grievances") if they feel it is acting unfairly.

States has a capitalist, free-market economy. This means that most businesses and goods are owned by private citizens, not by the government. The prices of products and services are based on how many goods are available, how much it costs to make them, and how much people are willing to pay for them.

In a capitalist economy, an individual can make a good living and even become rich. (For example, in a capitalist society, a person can become wealthy by starting a successful business or having an important job for a successful business.) In theory, any person living in a capitalist system can become rich, no matter what his or her background is. Yet many people living in capitalist societies remain poor, working for low wages. Some persons believe that the capitalist system is unfair. They feel that capitalism allows some people (owners of businesses) to achieve wealth at the expense of others (workers who are paid low wages by business owners).

RUSSIA AND THE SOVIET UNION

The Soviet Union (1922–1991) was a large group of states that covered much of eastern Europe and the entire northern half of Asia. While the history of the United States has often been marked by freedom and prosperity for many citizens, the history of the republics that made up the Soviet Union has been marked by brutal rule, poverty, and suffering. The USSR was dominated by its largest state, Russia.

In the 1500s, Russian czar (emperor) Ivan IV began passing a series of laws that gave the country's land to a small number of people who belonged to the ruling class.

Most Russians were farmers, who lived and worked on the land. Known as serfs, these farmers were forced to work for their owners and did not have the right to move from one place to the next. Serfs were, in fact, part of a landowner's property and were little more than slaves. (The word *serf* means "slave" in the Latin language.) Most lived in desperate poverty and had few rights under the law.

Over the next few centuries, the small Russian ruling class enjoyed fabulous wealth. But most of the Russian population suffered. At times, the serfs tried to overthrow their rulers. But government armies crushed these rebellions.

By the 1800s, movements to overthrow the Russian government were gathering strength. In response, Czar Alexander II freed the serfs in 1861. But these and other changes did not stop some Russians from

Miserable living conditions led Russian serfs to revolt against their rulers on several occasions. Here a group of serfs gathers around its leader during a revolt in 1773.

trying to destroy their government and replace it with a new one. These people formed political parties that called for a new and fairer kind of government.

One of these parties, the Bolshevik Party, demanded a completely new economic and political system for the country. Their new system was based on the ideas of a German-born writer named Karl Marx. Marx called for a society in which property belonged to the public, instead of to private individuals. In a Marxist society, businesses and farms would be owned by the people who worked in them. The government would provide housing, education, and health care for free. Instead of working to make a few people rich, everyone would work toward the common good. And everyone would share in the nation's wealth.

THE RUSSIAN REVOLUTION AND COMMUNISM

In 1914 Russia became involved in a massive and disastrous war in Europe. This war, which came to be known as World War I (1914–1918), weakened the country and its ruler, Czar Nicholas II. The cost of the war in both lives and money strained the country's economy to the breaking point. Food and fuel shortages created unrest among the public. In early 1917, Russian citizens staged violent strikes and protests throughout the country. To many of these Russians, Marx's ideas seemed like the solution to their troubles. Nicholas II was soon forced

> EYEWITNESS QUOTE:
> THE RUSSIAN REVOLUTION
>
> **"Yes, we are going to destroy everything [the old Russian rule], and on the ruins we will build our temple [a new Communist state]. It is a temple for the happiness of all!"**
>
> —**V. I. Lenin, describing the Russian Revolution**

to give up his rule. Late in 1917, the Bolshevik Party seized control of the Russian government.

Led by V. I. Lenin, the Bolshevik Party changed its name to the Communist Party. Lenin withdrew Russia from World War I, which ended in 1918. Over the next two years, Russia was torn by civil war. Communist troops, who came to be known as the "Red Army" (after the red Communist Party flag), fought against troops opposed to the Communist system, who were known as "the Whites." The United States and the

V. I. Lenin ordered the murder of Czar Nicholas II and his family. Lenin believed violence was the only way to win a Communist revolution in Russia.

1917г.
Дни революцiи.
Войска на Литейномъ просп.

Red Army soldiers during the early days of the Russian Revolution. The revolution and the civil war that followed caused tremendous destruction and death throughout Russia.

western European nations of Great Britain and France supported the Whites. These nations sent troops to try to defeat the Red Army. By 1920 the Communists had won control of the country. Lenin's government seized the nation's banks, railroads, and factories. Communist Party leaders took charge of these businesses.

THE RED SCARE AND AMERICAN COMMUNISM

These changes were alarming to many governments throughout the world, including the U.S. government. They feared that similar violent revolutions would spread to their countries.

In fact, the Russian Communists did have a worldwide revolution in mind. They believed that Communism would soon destroy capitalism. Lenin formed an inter-national organization to help Communist movements around the world. Known as the Communist International (Comintern), the organization sought to unite the world's Communist parties. The Comintern pro-vided international Communists with finan-cial support and leadership. Through the Comintern, the Russian Communists also controlled worldwide Communist move-ments. To receive support, international Communist leaders had to obey Soviet Communist orders.

Some Americans wanted to see a Communist revolution in the United States. They hoped such a change would lead to a better life for all Americans. These people formed the American Communist Party. Members of the party worked for better wages for workers. They also supported equal rights for minorities. The American

Communist Party was a member of the Comintern.

Because of this, U.S. leaders spoke out about the dangers of Communism, creating a wave of fear that spread across the country. This era came to be known as the "Red Scare." In 1920 the U.S. attorney general, A. Mitchell Palmer, the nation's top law-enforcement official, declared war on Communism.

A. Mitchell Palmer

He led a movement to deport, or throw out of the country, many American Communist Party members. Some Americans protested against these actions. They felt that by attacking Communists for their political opinions, Palmer was denying citizens their legal right to free speech.

Government attacks on the American Communist Party forced its leaders to go underground—to organize and meet in secret. Communist leaders also took on false names and identities and communicated in secret code.

THE BIRTH OF THE SOVIET UNION

In 1922 Lenin's Communist Party formed the Union of Soviet Socialist Republics. This was a confederation (united group) of four eastern European and western Asian states—Russia, Belarus, Ukraine, and Transcaucasia (modern-day Armenia,

> **EYEWITNESS QUOTE:**
> **THE RED SCARE**
>
> **"Like a prairie-fire, the blaze of revolution was sweeping over every American institution of law and order . . . burning up the foundations of society."**
>
> **—U.S. attorney general A. Mitchell Palmer**

Azerbaijan, and Georgia). The USSR's capital was in the Russian capital of Moscow.

In the early 1920s, the Soviet Union was chaotic. Years of civil war had left the country devastated. Many citizens were not getting the basic needs of life—food, clothing, and shelter. These hardships made some people question the promises of the Communist Party. Strikes and uprisings against the party erupted throughout the USSR. The Communists dealt violently with these revolts. Strike leaders were arrested and imprisoned. Many were executed.

The USSR had only one legal political party—the Communist Party. Other political groups were outlawed. Soviet citizens who spoke out against the Communists faced imprisonment, exile (forced removal from the country), or execution.

Meanwhile, the Soviet Union continued to expand in the early 1920s. Communist forces took control of a vast area in Central Asia (where modern-day Kazakhstan, Uzbekistan, Turkmenistan, Kyrgyzstan, and Tajikistan lie), dividing the area into several countries, which were included as Soviet Socialist Republics. The Communist Party in Moscow controlled these countries and their ruling Communist parties.

In 1924 Lenin died. Over the next few years, several Communist leaders tried to gain control of the country. By the end of the 1920s, one of these leaders—Joseph Stalin—

had become the ruler of the Communist Party and the Soviet Union itself.

STALIN AND TOTALITARIANISM

Throughout the late 1920s and the 1930s, Stalin worked ruthlessly to protect his rule. Soviets who criticized his policies (plans and ideas) were purged—murdered, imprisoned, or sent to Siberia, the Soviet Union's frozen northern wastelands. A secret police force spied on citizens who might be plotting against Stalin's rule. Most of the people who were suspected of treason (attempts to overthrow the government) were purged without trial in a court of law. By the late 1930s, Stalin and his followers had purged millions of Soviet citizens. The rest of the Soviet public lived in fear.

> **FAST FACT**
>
> **SIBERIA**
> Siberia is a frozen wasteland covering most of central and northern Russia. Temperatures there can drop below −90° F. Most of the Soviet Union's criminals and political prisoners were sent to the gulag (prison camps) in northeastern Siberia. Many prisoners died there of cold, starvation, and disease.

Soviet newspapers and magazines were controlled by the state. The government controlled book publishers as well. This meant that most Soviets only received news that praised the government and Communism and criticized capitalism. Schoolchildren often received a good education, but they

Soviet guards shackle the arms and legs of a prisoner in Siberia. In the 1930s, Stalin and his followers purged millions of Soviet citizens in a period known as the Great Terror.

Joseph Stalin

Joseph Stalin was born Iosif Vissarionovich Dzhugashvili on December 9, 1879, in the town of Gori in Georgia, a country located on the Black Sea. Raised in a poor peasant family, he studied to become a priest. But while in school, young Iosif learned about the revolutionary ideas of Karl Marx and joined a secret society of students who called for Georgian independence from Russian rule. Iosif was eventually expelled (thrown out) of school for his revolutionary views.

During the early 1900s, Iosif worked against Russian czarist rule, organizing strikes to protest government policies. The Russian government had him arrested, imprisoned, and then exiled to Siberia. He eventually made his way back to Georgia, where he joined V. I. Lenin's Bolsheviks. In 1913 he changed his name to Joseph Stalin, which roughly means "man of steel."

After the Bolsheviks seized power, Stalin held several key positions in the new government. After Lenin's death, Stalin beat out his rivals for the leadership of the Soviet Union. By 1929 he had become the dictator (total ruler) of the Soviet Union.

learned almost nothing about non-Communist ways of life. Stalin's power over his people was nearly total. This kind of government is known as totalitarianism.

THE GREAT DEPRESSION

Meanwhile, in the United States, the Great Depression changed the lives of most Americans. This period of severe economic hardship left millions of people out of work. Thousands of banks ran out of money and closed. Millions of people lost their life savings. Out of work and unable to pay their bills, many Americans were homeless and broke.

During these difficult years, some Americans found Communist ideas attractive. They saw Communism as a solution to the nation's problems. With so many people poor and desperate, the current system of government didn't seem to be working. Some felt that a revolution—a major change—was needed in the United States. In the mid-1930s, the American Communist Party made a major comeback. Membership grew from about 40,000 in 1936 to more than 82,000 in 1938.

Party groups helped the poor and needy. American Communists worked to organize labor unions that fought for workers' rights to fair pay and safer working conditions. Party members helped jobless workers to demand financial assistance from the government.

But these actions did not lead to any radical (extreme) changes in the U.S. government. Few Americans saw the need for a Communist revolution. Instead, the U.S. economy slowly improved in the late 1930s. As the Great Depression passed, the American Communist Party began to lose members.

WORLD WAR II

Meanwhile, in Europe, the nation of Germany was preparing for war. In the late 1930s, German leader Adolf Hitler had annexed (taken over) two of Germany's neighboring countries, Austria and Czechoslovakia. The rest of Europe feared Hitler's next move. On August 23, 1939, the Soviet Union signed a treaty (agreement) with Germany, the Molotov-Ribbentrop Pact. In it, both sides agreed not to interfere in the foreign affairs of the other. A few days later, on September 1, 1939, Germany invaded Poland from the west.

Several European nations, including Great Britain and France, declared war on Germany and its allies. This marked the beginning of World War II. On September 17, Soviet troops invaded Poland from the east. The Molotov-Ribbentrop Pact had called for Poland to be divided between Germany and the Soviet Union. By the end of September, the Soviet Union controlled one-third of Poland. Germany controlled the rest. Germany went on to conquer much of Europe and parts of North Africa.

Meanwhile, the United States remained neutral. It did not fight, but it supported Britain and its allies by lending them money and weapons.

In 1940 Stalin annexed the countries of Latvia, Estonia, and Lithuania, making them part of the USSR. Then in 1941, Hitler broke from the Molotov-Ribbentrop Pact. German forces invaded the Soviet Union. Months later, Germany's ally, the Pacific island nation of Japan, attacked the U.S. naval base at Pearl Harbor, in the Hawaiian Islands. The United States immediately declared war on Germany and Japan. Events had forced the United States and the Soviet Union to work together against

Soviet Red Army troops approach a bombed out building in the Russian city of Stalingrad in 1942. The Red Army suffered more than seven million combat deaths during World War II.

common enemies. The United States, the Soviet Union, and the countries that fought alongside them were known as the Allies.

At first, German forces slashed through the Soviet Union, causing terrible destruction and hundreds of thousands of deaths. Yet the Soviet Red Army gradually began to push back the Germans out of Eastern Europe. Meanwhile, the United States and the western Allies drove Germany out of North Africa and Western Europe. By early 1945, Allied troops had invaded Germany. Soviet troops took control of Czechoslovakia, Poland, Hungary, Romania, and other eastern nations that separated Germany from the Soviet Union. In the Pacific, the United States had scored huge victories against Japan. The Allies were on the verge of winning the war.

THE YALTA CONFERENCE

With Germany nearly defeated, the leaders of the three major Allied powers (the United States, the Soviet Union, and Great Britain) met in February 1945 to discuss what to do when the war ended. This conference took place in Soviet territory, at Yalta, a town on the Black Sea in the Ukraine. There Stalin met with U.S. president Franklin D. Roosevelt and British prime minister Winston Churchill.

The three leaders agreed on several issues. All supported the creation of an international peacekeeping organization. Such an organization would give countries a place to discuss their differences peacefully. This body would come to be known as the United Nations.

The "Big Three" Allied leaders *(seated, left to right)* Churchill, Roosevelt, and Stalin met at Yalta in February 1945. Roosevelt died two months after the conference.

The United Nations

The United Nations (UN) is an organization of nations that works for world peace and security, human rights, and to help fight hunger and disease. The UN was created near the end of World War II in hopes of preventing another global war.

The United Nations Charter was signed on June 26, 1945. By signing this document, all 50 founding nations agreed that they would try to settle disputes peacefully. They would also provide financial or military support for police actions—sending UN troops to keep peace in troubled regions. In the 2000s, most of the world's nations are members of the UN. The organization's main headquarters are in New York City.

The UN has several different parts, or organs. The largest organ, the General Assembly, controls all of the different UN branches. Actions taken by the General Assembly are based on votes by member nations, all of which send representatives to the General Assembly. Each member nation has one vote. Another organ, the Security Council, is a group of 15 countries that is responsible for dealing with issues of war and peace. Decisions for action by the council are based on council votes. The UN's International Court of Justice settles international legal disputes. The UN's Economic and Social Council directs agencies that work to improve its members' health and living conditions.

The closing session of the international conference during which the UN Charter was signed in 1945

The leaders also wanted to prevent Germany from becoming a military power again. So they agreed to divide Germany into four separate zones. Each of the zones would be occupied by one of the four victorious allies—Great Britain, the United States, the Soviet Union, and France. Allied troops would be stationed in these areas. The zones would be policed and governed by the Allies until the Germans could establish new governments in them. Stalin also agreed to begin fighting against Japan once Germany had surrendered.

The Allied leaders failed to reach an agreement on one issue, however. Soviet troops remained in control of Poland. Roosevelt and Churchill wanted Poland's prewar government returned to power. Stalin disagreed. In both World Wars, enemy invaders from the west had attacked his country from Poland. To make sure this never happened again, Stalin wanted a Soviet-friendly government to be in power there. Poland's prewar government was not likely to be pro-Soviet. After all, Soviet troops had invaded Poland in 1939. The leaders left Yalta with the issue of control of Poland unsettled.

In April President Roosevelt died. His vice president, Harry S. Truman, became president.

Weeks later, on May 8, 1945, Germany surrendered. The war in Europe was over.

THE POTSDAM CONFERENCE

By this time, Japan was on the verge of defeat. The Allied leaders again gathered to discuss the future. This conference took place in July 1945 in Potsdam, Germany. There, Stalin, Truman, and Churchill discussed the details of the future of Germany. (Midway through the conference, Churchill was defeated in the British national elections. The new British prime minister, Clement Attlee, replaced him at the conference on July 26.)

During the Potsdam Conference, President Truman received a message from the United States. U.S. scientists had successfully developed a powerful new super-weapon. Truman did not reveal what the weapon was. But he did declare in a public statement that Japan would face destruction if it did not surrender immediately.

At Potsdam major disagreements came up between the Soviets and the United States and Britain. Churchill, Attlee, and Truman accused Stalin of trying to set up Communist governments in the Eastern European countries where Soviet forces were stationed. Stalin wanted to make sure that friendly neighbors surrounded the Soviet Union. But Truman and the British leaders wanted the people of these nations to vote for their own governments. They accused Stalin of setting up "puppet" governments, whose leaders were under Soviet control.

THE ATOMIC BOMB

Despite Truman's statement at Potsdam, Japan refused to surrender. On August 6,

Harry S. Truman

Harry S. Truman was born in Lamar, Missouri, in 1884 and grew up in Independence, Missouri. Truman held many jobs as a young man, including bank clerk and farmer. After serving in the U.S. Army in World War I, Truman ran a clothing store in Kansas City, Missouri. Truman first ran for political office in the early 1920s and served in local government for many years before being elected to the U.S. Senate in 1934. President Roosevelt selected Truman as his vice presidential candidate for Roosevelt's victorious 1944 reelection campaign.

Truman had served as vice president for only 83 days when Roosevelt died in April 1945. Truman later described the shocking moment when he realized he had become president of the United States: "I felt like the moon, the stars, and all the planets had fallen on me." The new president had no experience in foreign affairs. Yet he was taking the most important job in the world at one of the most crucial periods in history.

The atomic bomb dropped on Hiroshima *(above)* created a blast *(inset)* that leveled much of the city, instantly killing tens of thousands of people. President Truman chose to drop the atomic bombs on Japan to avoid a U.S. invasion. U.S. military officials had predicted that an invasion of Japan would lead to approximately 500,000 U.S. combat deaths.

1945, the entire world learned about the United States' new superweapon—the atomic bomb. On that day, a U.S. bomber dropped a single atomic bomb on the Japanese city of Hiroshima. It created a massive explosion that leveled most of the city. Some 70,000 to 100,000 Japanese were killed. Three days later, a U.S. bomber dropped a second atomic bomb on Nagasaki, Japan. This bomb killed at least 40,000 people. Thousands more Japanese would later die from radiation poisoning caused by the blasts.

Japan agreed to surrender on August 14. The Japanese government signed formal surrender documents on September 2, 1945. World War II was over, and the United States and the Soviet Union had become the two most powerful nations on earth. But the distrust and suspicion between the two superpowers were growing. A new kind of war was brewing. It would come to be known as the Cold War.

FAST FACT

A single American bomber dropped the atomic bomb on Hiroshima, Japan. The bomb made a blast equal to about 13,000 tons of nonnuclear explosives. Delivering the same amount of explosive power in nonnuclear explosives would have required about 3,000 bombers. The explosion destroyed most of the city and killed about 70,000 to 100,000 people.

FROM ALLIES TO ENEMIES

2

At the end of the World War II, much of Europe lay in ruins. Millions of people had been killed in the fighting. Millions more were starving and homeless. Many cities had been reduced to rubble by bombing and ground battles. Farmland, factories, roads, and bridges had been destroyed.

In these desperate times, many Europeans found Communist ideas attractive. The horrors of the war led many to believe that their old governments had failed them. More and more Europeans began to look to Communism as a new—perhaps better—way of life. In Western Europe, Communist parties grew in strength as more and more people joined them. In Eastern Europe, the Soviet Union placed Soviet-friendly Communists in power.

Following the Potsdam Conference, Stalin continued to exercise control over his Eastern European neighbors. In the years following the war, he set up new governments in Poland, Hungary, Romania, Bulgaria, Czechoslovakia, and the Soviet zone of Germany. These countries came to be known as the Eastern Bloc (group).

EYEWITNESS QUOTE:
EUROPE IN RUINS

"[European] housing [was] often wrecked buildings. . . . Workers went on strike because they weren't being paid. The communist parties, particularly in France and Italy, were growing in size. They held enormous demonstrations, which paralyzed the streets."

—U.S. official
Theodore Geiger

The Iron Curtain

The roughly geographical dividing line between the Communist countries of Eastern Europe and the Western democracies became known as the Iron Curtain. Former British prime minister Winston Churchill coined this phrase during a famous speech at Westminster College in Missouri on March 5, 1946:

> An iron curtain has descended across the Continent [of Europe]. Behind that line lie all the capitals of the ancient states of Central and Eastern Europe. Warsaw, Berlin, Prague, Vienna, Budapest, Belgrade, Bucharest and Sofia, all these famous cities and the populations around them lie in what I must call the Soviet sphere, and all are subject in one form or another . . . to Soviet influence.

Eastern Bloc governments were ruled by Communist parties that took their orders from Moscow. By creating a buffer zone of Communist nations in Eastern Europe, the Soviet Union was protecting itself from invasion from the West.

The leaders of the Western democracies were alarmed by Stalin's actions. They had wanted all of Europe to be independent, democratic, and capitalist. Western leaders believed that these nations should have the right to govern themselves. They also believed that citizens should have the right to vote for their own leaders. Western leaders were confident that, if given a choice, countries would not choose Communism. Yet the Eastern Bloc nations did not have a choice.

Western leaders were also concerned that Stalin might try to extend his control beyond the Eastern Bloc. They began to develop a plan to keep Stalin from further spreading his influence in Europe. This policy became known as containment. Its goal was to contain, or limit, the power and influence of the Soviet Union and Communism.

THE TRUMAN DOCTRINE AND THE MARSHALL PLAN

President Truman introduced the strategy of containment in a speech on March 12, 1947. Speaking to the U.S. Congress, Truman declared, "It must be the policy of the United States to support free peoples who are resisting attempted subjugation [conquest] by armed minorities or by outside pressures." This plan for containment would come to be known as the Truman Doctrine.

> **EYEWITNESS QUOTE: THE SPREAD OF COMMUNISM**
>
> "I am more convinced than ever that communism is on the march on a worldwide scale, which only America can stop."
>
> —U.S. senator Arthur Vandenberg, 1946

Yet U.S. leaders wanted to contain Communism without having to go to war. They looked for financial ways—instead of military ways—to limit Communism. U.S. leaders knew that Europe needed help to rebuild. By helping them to do this, they believed European nations would support the United States and its democratic form of government.

On June 5, 1947, the U.S. secretary of state, George C. Marshall, announced what came to be called the Marshall Plan. This program offered billions of dollars in aid to nations that were recovering from World War II. It was also designed to help stop the spread of Communism. In announcing the plan, Marshall said:

George C. Marshall

> Our policy is directed not against any country or doctrine, but against hunger, poverty, desperation and chaos. . . . Any government that is willing to assist in the task of recovery will find full co-operation. . . . Any government which [blocks] the recovery of other countries cannot expect help from us.

Advertising the Marshall Plan

The U.S. Congress wanted Europeans to know that the United States was helping them to rebuild after the war. Officials put up posters advertising the Marshall Plan throughout participating countries. Goods shipped under the plan—food, clothing, medical supplies, building supplies, farming equipment, and countless other items—were clearly marked. Early labels said, "For European Recovery—Supplied by the United States of America." In later years, the labels were changed to "Strength for the Free World—from the United States of America."

FOR EUROPEAN RECOVERY
SUPPLIED BY THE
UNITED STATES OF AMERICA

The Marshall Plan was available to any European country that wanted to participate. But the Soviet government saw the program as a threat to its own power in Eastern Europe. The Soviets claimed that the United States was trying to control Europe by making it depend on U.S. money. Soviet foreign minister Vyacheslav Molotov said that the plan would divide "Europe into two groups of states . . . creating new difficulties in the relations between them." The Soviet Union and the rest of the Eastern Bloc refused to participate in the Marshall Plan.

DISPUTES OVER GERMANY

As 1947 ended, tensions between East and West continued to grow. The two sides debated Germany's long-term future. The United States and Britain wanted to see Germany reunited as a democratic state. Soviet leaders feared that a revived Germany might again wage war against the USSR.

When the two sides could not reach an agreement, the Western powers decided to work without the Soviet Union. In June 1948, the United States, Great Britain, and France announced that the three German zones under their control would be united as a new nation. This country would come to be known as the Federal Republic of Germany, or West Germany. The sector (section) of Germany under Soviet control would not be included in this new country.

Soviet leaders saw this decision as a violation of agreements made at the Potsdam Conference. They responded by trying to force the Western powers out of Germany's former capital, Berlin.

Berlin, Germany's largest city, lies in the heart of eastern Germany. After Germany's defeat, Berlin—like Germany itself—was divided into occupation zones controlled by the Allies. Soviet forces occupied eastern Berlin. U.S., British, and French troops controlled the western part of the city. The two areas of the divided city became known as East Berlin and West Berlin. Yet all of Berlin lay within the Soviet occupation zone. People from the West had to travel through Soviet-occupied territory to reach West Berlin.

On June 24, 1948, the Soviets created a blockade, closing all highway, rail, and water traffic routes between West Germany and West Berlin. This meant that West Berlin was completely cut off from food and fuel. By doing this, the Soviets hoped that the Western powers would give up West Berlin to Soviet control.

The United States, Great Britain, and France had a dangerous problem. They did not want to give in to the Soviet Union's illegal move. They did not want to give up West Berlin. The policy of containment was being put to the test.

West Berlin's two million citizens relied on the Western powers for food, fuel, medical supplies, and other necessities. Cut off from the West, the city faced starvation. But sending soldiers in to fight through the blockade might be disastrous. Such a move could start World War III.

Instead, the American and British military leaders came up with a different idea. They decided to go over the blockade. Every available American and British cargo (supply) airplane was called upon to help in a massive airlift. Starting June 26, planes from West Germany began flying supplies over the Soviet sector and into West Berlin. Within weeks, tons of supplies were being shipped to the blockaded city each day, in what came to be known as the Berlin Airlift. At the same time, the Western powers began their own blockade. This counterblockade stopped shipments of valuable coal and steel from the West to the Eastern Bloc.

As months passed, the situation became a test of wills. Who would back down first, the West or the Soviets? By December

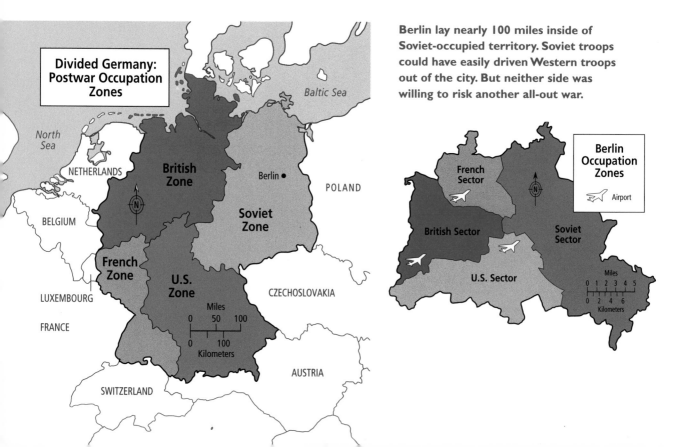

Divided Germany: Postwar Occupation Zones

Baltic Sea

North Sea

NETHERLANDS

British Zone

Berlin ●

POLAND

Soviet Zone

BELGIUM

French Zone

U.S. Zone

CZECHOSLOVAKIA

LUXEMBOURG

FRANCE

Miles
0   50   100

0   100
Kilometers

AUSTRIA

SWITZERLAND

Berlin lay nearly 100 miles inside of Soviet-occupied territory. Soviet troops could have easily driven Western troops out of the city. But neither side was willing to risk another all-out war.

Berlin Occupation Zones

✈ Airport

French Sector

British Sector

Soviet Sector

U.S. Sector

Miles
0 1 2 3 4 5

0   2   4   6
Kilometers

Children in Berlin watch as a cargo plane flies overhead during the Berlin Airlift. Many of the airlift pilots were ex-bomber pilots who had bombed the city during World War II.

1948, hundreds of American and British planes were making round-the-clock flights. Aircraft landed every 90 seconds during peak periods.

By the spring of 1949, the Berlin Airlift was still going strong. The West was showing no sign of giving in. And the counterblockade was damaging East Germany's rebuilding efforts. The Soviet Union finally backed down and lifted the blockade in May. The West had won the first "battle" of the Cold War.

THE BERLIN AIRLIFT
During the 10-month Berlin Airlift, a total of 278,228 flights carried 2,326,406 tons of supplies to the isolated city. Supplies included coal for heating, flour for baking bread, clothing, and blankets.

FAST FACT

THE NORTH ATLANTIC TREATY

The confrontation over Germany was a major turning point in Western-Soviet relations. The controversy pushed the two sides farther apart. By early 1949, it was clear that the Soviet Union would rule the Eastern Bloc for many years. Western leaders decided to create an alliance (union) that could equal the strength of the Eastern Bloc.

On April 4, 1949, the United States, Canada, and 10 Western European countries signed the North Atlantic Treaty. This treaty created the North Atlantic Treaty Organization (NATO). NATO's countries agreed to treat an attack on one member as an attack on all members. The North Atlantic Treaty divided Europe. The alliance created a political balance of power between East and West. Backed by the power of the United States, the rest of the NATO countries believed that the Soviet Union and the Eastern Bloc countries would not attack Western Europe.

Yet the United States had a major military advantage in the Cold War—the atomic bomb. At this point, only the United States possessed this new superweapon. Western leaders believed the Soviet Union would not dare attack NATO members for fear of an atomic counterattack.

But the West's sense of security did not last for long. Less than five months after the North Atlantic Treaty was signed, the

Soviets successfully tested their own atomic bomb. Suddenly, the West's advantage had disappeared. The military balance of power had shifted. People living in both East and West lived in fear of nuclear war.

In response, Truman and his advisers stepped up plans to create a new kind of nuclear bomb. This bomb, called a hydrogen bomb, would be 1,000 times more powerful than the atomic bombs dropped on Hiroshima and Nagasaki. A race to create the most powerful weapons—an arms race—was under way.

A NEW
3 RED SCARE

In the years following World War II, a new Red Scare swept across the United States. As the Soviet Union established its control in Eastern Europe, many Americans feared Communists were also trying to take over the United States.

Years earlier, Congress had formed the House Un-American Activities Committee (HUAC). This group of U.S. senators and representatives investigated Americans suspected of treason against the United States. HUAC's main purpose was to go after suspected spies, or people who might be passing along military secrets to the nation's enemies.

But the committee often went much further. After World War II, HUAC began a major crackdown on Communism. Instead of just going after spies, it worked to completely destroy Communism in the United States.

HUAC worked with the Federal Bureau of Investigation (FBI), the United States' national law enforcement agency. FBI agents spied on suspected Communists. To do this, the FBI broke the law. The U.S. Constitution says that people have the right to privacy, "to be secure in their persons, houses, papers, and effects, against unreasonable searches..." Yet FBI agents illegally "tapped" phone lines, listening to conversations between suspects. They also placed bugs—hidden microphones—in homes and offices of suspected "Reds."

Agents broke into homes and offices to look for damaging evidence.

The crackdown on Communism caused many Americans to fear their government. This fear kept many from expressing their political views unless they were strongly anti-Communist. Yet dissent—criticism of the government—is a guaranteed right under the Constitution.

THE HOLLYWOOD TEN

In 1947 HUAC turned its attention to Hollywood, California, the center of the American movie industry. HUAC members looked for actors, writers, and film directors who might be Communists. HUAC believed that some filmmakers were producing films that had pro-Communist messages. They feared that these films—watched by millions of Americans—would influence people into becoming Communists.

In the fall of 1947, HUAC called on 43 witnesses to testify in front of the committee about Communism in Hollywood. HUAC knew that more than half of these people were strongly anti-Communist and would cooperate with the committee. These friendly witnesses spoke about the

Hollywood screenwriter Dalton Trumbo (*center*), a member of the Hollywood Ten and a Communist, refused to cooperate with HUAC. He was soon banned from working in the movie industry. Yet Trumbo continued to secretly write movie scripts under a false name. He even won an Academy Award in 1956. Other suspected Communists struggled to find work in Hollywood for many years.

problems Communism was causing in the movie industry. They also congratulated HUAC for its work in fighting Communism. The friendly witnesses were movie producers, writers, and some famous actors, including a popular actor named Ronald Reagan.

HUAC also chose people whom they thought would be unfriendly witnesses. The committee believed that most of these persons were Communists or ex-Communists. Ten of them appeared before HUAC. Each was expected to answer the question, "Are you now, or have you ever been, a member of the Communist Party?"

The unfriendly witnesses had three choices, all of them difficult. They could deny their Communist Party connections. But lying to the committee was a crime for which they could be sent to prison. A second choice was to admit that they had been Communists. But if they did this, they risked being fired from their jobs.

The Hollywood Ten, as they came to be called, chose a third option—they refused to answer HUAC's questions. The Hollywood Ten wanted to stand up to HUAC. They wanted to show the country that HUAC was unfair and unlawful. According to the First Amendment, the committee had no legal right to ask them about their political beliefs. It was no one's business whether or not they were Communists.

> ### EYEWITNESS QUOTE: THE HOLLYWOOD TEN
>
> "I didn't do anything when I was in [the American Communist] Party, I mean that. . . . Nothing really happened at Party meetings. Mainly, we discussed what was going on in the world. . . . We talked about the political situation and what was going on. They were all good things, what could we do to improve housing, or to improve the racial attitudes of the people."
>
> —Edward Dmytryk, one of the Hollywood Ten

One by one, the Hollywood Ten were questioned by HUAC. Each refused to answer the committee's questions. Instead, they challenged the committee's right to even ask about their political beliefs. They hoped that the public, which was watching the meetings on TV, would stand behind them and realize that HUAC was unfair.

But they were wrong. While some Americans did sympathize with the Hollywood Ten, most did not. Most Americans were more concerned about the spread of Communism than they were concerned about losing constitutional rights.

Refusing to answer HUAC's questions angered committee members. They charged each of the Ten with contempt of Congress—breaking the laws of the U.S. Congress. Each of the Hollywood Ten was sentenced to prison for six months to a year.

Hollywood was stunned. Movie industry leaders worried about the public's reaction. Would they think that Hollywood was full of Communists? If so, they feared Americans might stop going to movies. Industry leaders decided to "clean up" Hollywood.

In November 1947, Hollywood's top leaders announced that they would not "knowingly employ [hire] a Communist or a member of any party or group which [supported] the overthrow of the Government of the United States by force, or by any illegal or unconstitutional methods." All of

the Hollywood Ten were fired from their jobs. They and other suspected Communists were blacklisted (banned) from working in the movie industry.

Hollywood was not the only place where blacklists appeared. Government employees, university employees, factory workers, even schoolteachers were at risk of being fired for their political beliefs as the Red Scare swept across the nation.

SPIES

The Red Scare became worse when the Soviets set off their first atomic bomb in 1949. U.S. leaders had predicted it would take the Soviets at least a few more years to build their own bomb. How had they done the job so quickly? Some Americans wondered if spies had given the Soviets secrets about building nuclear weapons. So the U.S. government launched a massive spy hunt.

The suspicions were correct. A few months after the first Soviet bomb was exploded, a British scientist named Klaus Fuchs was arrested in London. Fuchs had worked on the program that developed the first American atomic bomb during World War II. The scientist confessed to passing secret atomic information to the Soviets. Soviet scientists had used Fuchs's information to speed up the process of building a nuclear bomb. Fuchs also named other people who had helped the Soviets. More arrests were made, and more spies were uncovered. Fuchs was sentenced to fourteen years in prison.

The case of one suspected spy caused a sensation in the United States. An electrical engineer named Julius Rosenberg was

Klaus Fuchs was a brilliant scientist. British and U.S. officials had ignored his Communist past to gain his help in building the atomic bomb.

accused of passing important scientific information to the Soviets during World War II. The FBI had evidence that Rosenberg was a Communist.

Rosenberg refused to confess or to name other Soviet agents (spies). So the government charged his wife, Ethel, with espionage (spying) too. U.S. officials hoped this would persuade Julius Rosenberg to confess to his crimes, but he remained silent.

On the surface, the legal case against the Rosenbergs appeared weak. U.S. law enforcement officials seemed to have very little proof of the Rosenbergs' guilt. Instead, the government relied on confessions of jailed spies, including Julius Rosenberg's brother-in-law. Many Americans wondered if these witnesses could be trusted. They might have been cooperating with the government to shorten their own prison sentences. Nevertheless, Julius and Ethel Rosenberg were found guilty of espionage on March 29, 1951, and sentenced to execution.

The Rosenberg case attracted world-wide attention. For some, the case showed that anti-Communism was out of control in America. Famous people, such as the Pope and scientist Albert Einstein, had called for the couple's release. Some Rosenberg supporters pointed out that he had given the Soviets the information when the two countries were allies during the war. Did this make him an enemy? Yet many Americans supported the Rosenbergs' execution. They felt that Soviet spies were a threat to the United States and should be shown no mercy. Julius and Ethel Rosenberg were executed on June 19, 1953.

The Venona Documents

New evidence about the Julius and Ethel Rosenberg spy case surfaced in 1995 when the U.S. government released the Venona documents. These top-secret reports showed proof of Soviet spy activity in the United States during the 1940s. During World War II, U.S. agents had kept close track of Soviet communications to and from the United States. These agents read coded telegrams between the Soviet Union and Soviet spies in the United States. The telegrams showed that Julius Rosenberg

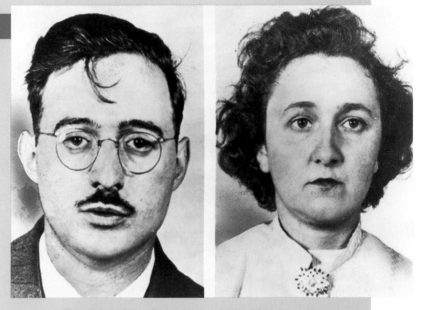

The trial of the Rosenbergs (*above*) became a symbol of the Red Scare of the 1950s.

had, in fact, been a Soviet spy. Ethel was also mentioned in one message. But no evidence of her guilt appears in the Venona documents.

U.S. officials probably knew about the Venona documents during the Rosenberg trial. But they did not make this information public at the time. This was because U.S. officials did not want the Soviets to know they had cracked their secret codes.

SPIES AND SPYING

While U.S. and Soviet armies never clashed during the Cold War, people on both sides of the conflict did risk—and sometimes lose—their lives fighting the enemy. Espionage—spying on the enemy—played an important role in the Cold War, as the United States and the Soviet Union used secret agents and cutting-edge technology to try to learn one another's secrets.

Spy agencies During the Cold War, both the United States and the Soviet Union used agencies for gathering intelligence (information) about foreign governments and militaries. In 1947 President Truman signed a law creating the Central Intelligence Agency (CIA). The CIA gathers intelligence about foreign governments, leaders, and militaries, using spies, technology such as spy satellites, and researchers who closely read foreign and U.S. publications for information. In the Soviet Union, the major intelligence agency was the Committee for State Security, known by its Russian initials, KGB.

Spies Some spies tried to uncover the enemy's military secrets—such as the number of troops and weapons the enemy had, where they were located, and what the enemy was planning to do with them. Others tried to steal and pass on information on military technology. During the early Cold War years, the only way to get this information was to either send spies into enemy territory to work undercover or—more often—to recruit from the enemy people in important positions. One such recruit, Oleg Penkovsky, was a high-ranking Soviet officer. Penkovsky passed important information to Western agents about Soviet missile developments, nuclear plans, and the locations of Soviet military headquarters. Penkovsky was caught in late 1962 and executed several months later.

Some spies seduced—romanced—people who could get the information they wanted. For example, in Germany in the early 1960s, a young Soviet-trained spy, Heinz Suetterlin, won the heart of Leonora Heinz, a young woman who worked for the West German government. Suetterlin convinced Leonora to steal secret government documents, which Suetterlin copied and passed on to Communist agents. After several years, Suetterlin and Leonora were caught.

Other intelligence roles

- Double agents are spies who switch sides—for example, a KGB agent who is recruited to work for the CIA. A double agent can be doubly dangerous, because an agent that switches sides can continue to feed false information to his or her old agency.
- Couriers pass secret information from one agent to another, often at great risk.
- Moles are agents working within the enemy's agency—for example, a KGB agent working within the CIA. The term "mole" comes from a kind of rodent

that lives underground. Moles can be especially dangerous because they often have access to very valuable secret information.

- Assassins carry out murders of important enemies—for example, dissident leaders or enemy agents—often within enemy territory.
- Interrogators often use torture to gain information from captured enemies.

Spy tools Espionage is a dangerous business. Spies are constantly at risk of being captured, so they need to keep their activities a secret. Spy agencies have developed many clever tools to help spies keep their work undercover.

- Microfilm and microdots are used to store important secret documents in very small packages so they can be carried and passed on to couriers with less risk of detection. A single microdot photo is less than 1/16th of a square inch.

- Spy cameras are used to photograph secret documents, secret weapons, military sites, etc. Since secrecy was crucial, agents hid cameras in everyday objects. Secret spy cameras were placed in special cigarette packs, cigarette lighters, neckties, watches, briefcases, purses, and books.
- Bugs are listening devices—usually tiny microphones—that can be hidden in telephones, lamps, walls, and just about anywhere else. Agents "bugged" homes, businesses, government buildings, and other locations.
- Spy weapons are used for assassinations and/or self-defense. To escape detection, agencies created tiny guns that could be hidden in many everyday items. Spies carried guns in cigarette packs, in pens, in flashlights, and even tiny pistols that could be rolled in cigarette paper to look like cigarettes. Some of these weapons fired bullets. Others shot poison pellets or sprayed poison gas.

Soviet agents hid microfilm messages in hollow shaving brushes, nails, pencils, and cuff links.

- Suicide devices were given to spies operating in enemy territory. Some spies chose to kill themselves rather than be captured and tortured by interrogators.

In the 1950s, some important spying tasks were taken over by new technology—in particular, spy planes and spy satellites. Spy planes such as the U-2 were able to fly over Soviet territory and photograph military sites. Spy satellites—developed in the early 1960s—performed the same role hundreds of miles above the earth. But these new machines could not uncover many of the secrets that only spies working inside an organization could find. Thus spies played an important role throughout the Cold War and beyond.

McCARTHYISM

Some U.S. politicians used the wave of anti-Communist panic to get attention. The most famous of these was Joseph McCarthy, a U.S. senator from Wisconsin. On February 9, 1950, the senator made a speech in which he claimed to have a list of 205 government workers who were members of the American Communist Party. His speech caused a sensation. Was the government really full of Communists? Were they plotting to take over the country?

The nation wanted to know more. But when asked for details, McCarthy kept changing his story. The day after his first speech, the number of Communists had dropped to 57. Ten days later, the number he gave to the U.S. Senate was 81. McCarthy didn't seem very trustworthy, but fear still led many senators to support him. No one wanted to be labeled "soft"—not tough—on Communism.

McCarthy made headlines with his wild approach to anti-Communism. He used rough language and bullied witnesses. This style of attacking people came to be known as "McCarthyism."

As time passed, McCarthy's accusations became bolder. In 1951 he attacked former secretary of state George C. Marshall. He delivered a long speech accusing Marshall of betraying Eastern Europe to the Communists. Many Americans were outraged that McCarthy would attack such a

> **EYEWITNESS QUOTE:**
> **THE RED MENACE**
>
> "Communism, in reality, is not a political party, it is a way of life, an evil and malignant [deadly] way of life. It reveals a condition [similar] to a disease that spreads like an epidemic and like an epidemic a quarantine is necessary to keep it from infecting this nation."
>
> —J. Edgar Hoover, director, Federal Bureau of Investigation

respected person who had done so much for the United States.

McCarthy's wild charges earned him a growing list of enemies. One of these enemies, Dwight D. Eisenhower, became president in January 1953. But even the popular new president would not publicly criticize McCarthy. With the public still worried about the threat of Communism, Eisenhower did not want to appear soft. Nor did he want to sink to McCarthy's crude level. "I will not . . . get in the gutter with that guy," Eisenhower explained. Instead, he kept silent and waited for the senator to make a mistake.

It did not take long for this to happen. In the summer of 1953, McCarthy earned another powerful enemy, J. Edgar Hoover, director of the FBI. For years Hoover had given McCarthy evidence on Communist activity in the United States. This information had helped to fuel McCarthy's investigations. But as McCarthy became more careless, Hoover stopped supporting him. Without evidence provided by the FBI, McCarthy had very little information with which to attack Communists.

J. Edgar Hoover

By this time, McCarthy had begun investigating Communists in the U.S. Army. McCarthy set up a series of hearings (meetings where witnesses are called to speak) that were broadcast on live television. According to historian Ellen Schrecker, "For two months, the nation watched the Wisconsin senator repeatedly disrupt the proceedings . . . in order to bully witnesses, deliver lectures, and make crude and insulting remarks."

The big moment came a month into the hearings. On June 9, McCarthy made wild charges against someone who wasn't even involved in the hearings. Joseph Welch, a man representing the army, defended the person McCarthy had accused. Welch lashed back at McCarthy with a famous response:

Until this moment, Senator, I think I never really gauged your cruelty or your recklessness. . . . Let us not assassinate this lad further, Senator. You have done enough. Have you no sense of decency, sir, at long last? Have you left no sense of decency?

Welch seemed to be saying what was on many American minds. McCarthy showed the ugly side of anti-Communism. More and more citizens began to question McCarthy and his methods. At the same time, important public leaders began speaking

With his mean-spirited style, Senator Joseph McCarthy (center) earned national attention and many powerful enemies. McCarthy's attacks on the U.S. Army led to his downfall.

out against the senator. On December 2, 1954, the U.S. Senate passed a censure motion—a statement of strong disapproval—condemning McCarthy's ruthless ways. Two years later, he failed to be reelected to the U.S. Senate. McCarthy vanished from the public scene and died from alcoholism in 1957.

Overall, though, HUAC succeeded in its anti-Communist campaign. "McCarthyism had set out to eradicate [get rid of] Communism from American society," wrote Schrecker, "and it did." By the end of the 1950s, the American Communist Party was in ruins.

Historians still debate how much of a threat Communism was to American society. Were American Communists really seeking to overthrow the government? Some did have such a goal. And many high-level American Communists did take orders from the Soviet Union. A handful of American Communists were, in fact, spies, passing on secret information to the Soviet Union. But most American Communists were simply hardworking people who wanted a better life for themselves and their families. To them, Communism's promise to give power to the working person was very appealing. Yet many lost their jobs and had their reputations destroyed because of their involvement with the Communist Party.

> ### EYEWITNESS QUOTE: HOUNDING COMMUNISTS
>
> "[Publicly stating that I was a Communist] caused a lot of controversy and a lot of threats. . . . I was watched by the FBI twenty-four hours a day for years. I remember in 1950 the FBI would follow me . . . two or three carloads of them. . . . I'd have a dozen guys encircling me, moving as I moved. . ."
>
> **Junius Scales, American Communist**

Dwight D. Eisenhower

Dwight D. Eisenhower was born on October 14, 1890, in Denison, Texas, and was raised in Abilene, Kansas. He was the supreme commander of Allied forces in Europe and North Africa during much of World War II. In this post, he was credited with getting the many different Allied commanders to work together to defeat Germany. Ike, as he was often called, took over supreme command of NATO in 1951. Eisenhower's reputation as a war hero helped him easily win election as the president of the United States in 1952.

COMMUNISM
4 ON THE MARCH

In October 1949, a Communist government had come to power in China, the world's most populous nation. Months later, Stalin and Chinese Communist leader Mao Zedong signed a treaty of friendship and military cooperation. These events greatly alarmed U.S. leaders. Communism seemed to be spreading around the world. How could it be contained in Asia? A few months later, the containment policy would be put to the test. The challenge came on the Korean Peninsula, in northeast Asia.

A DIVIDED KOREA

North Korea and South Korea occupy a peninsula (a piece of land that juts out from a larger piece of land) in northeastern

Asia, just west of the islands of Japan. Korea was under Japanese control from 1895 until Japan's defeat in World War II. After the war, Soviet forces occupied the northern half of Korea, while U.S. forces occupied the southern half. The two halves were divided along the 38th Parallel, a line of latitude (an imaginary line that runs parallel to the equator) that roughly cuts the country in half.

In the north, the Soviets helped Kim Il Sung, a Communist, take control of the government. The United States backed Syngman Rhee, an anti-Communist leader, to rule the south. Each leader wanted to reunify the country. But neither side wanted to share power.

In January 1948, the United Nations called for free elections throughout Korea. But the Soviets and North Korean leaders refused to cooperate. Elections were held only in South Korea, and Syngman Rhee was elected president of the Republic of Korea. In September the North Korean Communists created the Democratic People's Republic of Korea. Each government claimed to be the government of all of Korea. The two sides fought a few short battles along the 38th Parallel.

By mid-1949, Soviet and U.S. forces had withdrawn from Korea. By early 1950, the North Korean Communists were working on a plan to invade the south. Encouraged by Stalin and Mao, the Communists did not think the United States would try to stop them. Mao believed the Americans "would not start a third world war over such a small territory."

THE KOREAN WAR

On June 25, 1950, the North Korean army invaded the south. The United Nations immediately demanded that North Korea withdraw to its own territory. But the North Koreans ignored this demand and continued to march southward. By June 27, Communist forces had come within range of the South Korean capital of Seoul. That same day, President Truman ordered U.S. forces to the area to defend South Korea.

The Communists had gambled that the United States would not be willing to fight to contain Communism. But U.S. leaders, backed by the United Nations, stood firm. The United Nations voted to send military aid to South Korea. Forty-one UN member countries sent supplies, food, or military equipment. Sixteen UN member countries

The United Nations Security Council and the Korean War

In 1950 the United States, the Soviet Union, Great Britain, and France all held permanent seats on the UN Security Council. As permanent members, they had the right to veto (strike down) any decision made by the rest of the Security Council.

In June 1950, the council voted to send troops to Korea to stop the North Korean invasion of South Korea. The Soviet Union, which supported the North Koreans, disagreed with this decision. The action could have been vetoed by the Soviets, but they did not vote. At the time, the Soviet Union was boycotting (refusing to participate in) the Security Council for other reasons. Without the Soviet vote, the United Nations was able to support the Korean War.

joined the United States in sending troops to defend South Korea. Meanwhile, the Soviet Union and China supplied North Korea with weapons and equipment.

The first months of the war saw dramatic shifts. By September 1950, North Korean forces had almost completely overrun the South. But once UN forces had arrived in large numbers, they counterattacked. UN forces pushed deep into North Korea. By October the Communists were close to defeat. Then Mao Zedong stepped in to save them, sending hundreds of thousands of Chinese troops to fight alongside the North Koreans. By January 1951, the North Koreans and Chinese had pushed the UN forces back below the 38th Parallel. A few months later, UN troops pushed the Communists north again.

By the spring of 1951, both sides had dug in along a line north of the 38th Parallel. Peace talks began in July, but the two sides continued to fight.

The Korean War, as it came to be called, was a new kind of war. For the first time in its short history, the United Nations sent troops to fight for one country against another, and for the first time, Western nations used military force to keep Communism from spreading.

The Korean War was also a limited war. Both the Communists and the non-Communists made sure that the fighting did not spread to other countries. The horrors of World War II, which had ended just five years earlier, were still fresh in everyone's minds. Neither side wanted to start World War III.

The Korean War finally ended on July 27, 1953, when an armistice agreement was signed between North Korea and the United Nations. In 1954 representatives from North and South Korea met in Geneva, Switzerland, to discuss reunifying the country. But no solution was reached. Korea remains divided between the Communist North and the democratic South.

Korean War 1950–1953

CHINA

Chinese Intervention October 1950

Farthest advance by UN Forces November 1950

Chongju

NORTH KOREA

⊕ Pyongyang

Armistice Line July 27, 1953

Miles
0 25 50 75
0 50 100
Kilometers

38th Parallel

⊕ Seoul

Farthest advance by Chinese and North Korean Forces January 1951

SEA OF JAPAN

Farthest advance by North Korean Forces September 1950

YELLOW SEA

SOUTH KOREA

JAPAN

THE HOMEFRONT

Duck and Cover

News that the Soviet Union had developed its own atomic bomb in 1949 unleashed a wave of panic across the United States. In the early 1950s, millions of Americans rushed to build "bomb shelters" in hopes of surviving a nuclear war. These shelters were often cement brick rooms built underground or within the basement of houses. Builders offered a wide range of bomb shelters, from cheap, tiny $13.50 holes in the ground to fancy $5,000 models with a telephone, beds, toilets, and even a Geiger counter—a device used for measuring radiation.

In January 1951, President Truman signed a law creating the Federal Civil Defense Administration (FCDA) to educate the American public on how to survive a nuclear war. The FCDA provided learning materials to

American schoolchildren practice a duck-and-cover drill.

schools and homes about what to do in the event of a nuclear attack. The FCDA's most famous creation was Bert the Turtle, a cartoon turtle who demonstrated "duck and cover"—the drill of dropping to the floor or ground and covering your head during a nuclear attack. Most American kids growing up in the 1950s performed duck-and-cover drills on a regular basis. Usually, these drills involved students dropping to the floor and lying face down under their desks. Some large U.S. cities gave out identification tags to all students to be worn at all times. The tags were meant to be used to identify those killed (and burned beyond recognition) in a nuclear war.

The development of hydrogen bombs made nearly all bomb shelters worthless. Not only were the new weapons powerful enough to destroy nearly any structure, they created massive amounts of radioactive fallout, the poisonous radioactive material created by a nuclear explosion. In response to the new threat, some Americans built "fallout shelters," which they hoped would allow them to survive until the fallout cleared. But fallout from a full-scale nuclear war would have hovered in the earth's atmosphere for months, creating a "nuclear winter" that would poison nearly all the world's plants, animals, and people. Those who might be lucky enough to survive a nuclear war and a long nuclear winter would find very little life left in the world.

CHANGES IN LEADERSHIP

During the Korean War, both the United States and the Soviet Union saw changes in leadership. In the United States, Dwight D. Eisenhower had been elected president. Stalin had died from a stroke (a burst blood vessel in his brain). The man who had ruled the Soviet Union with an iron fist for 30 years had never made plans for anyone to replace him. The nation was thrown into turmoil as several top Communist leaders competed to rule the nation.

The West eagerly waited for the results of the Soviet power struggle. Many Westerners hoped that the new Soviet premier would be easier to work with than the hardheaded Stalin. Over the next five years, the post changed hands, as different men competed for control of the country. During this time, one man began to emerge as the Soviet Union's leading figure—Nikita Khrushchev.

Nikita Khrushchev

Just months after Stalin's death, Khrushchev became head of the Soviet Union's Communist Party. From this high-level job, he worked to become premier.

Khrushchev was very different from Stalin. Stalin had been a quiet, calm person. Khrushchev was excitable and outspoken. Western leaders saw him as unpredictable. But Khrushchev, like the other Soviet leaders who came after Stalin, believed that better relations with the West would benefit the Soviet Union. In July 1955, Khrushchev and Eisenhower met in Geneva. Many world leaders viewed the summit (meeting of top leaders) as a "big thaw" in the Cold War. In February 1956, Khrushchev announced that he wanted East and West to live peacefully together. He wanted each side to "live and let live."

Still, the arms race continued. In the early 1950s, the Soviet Union and the United States had both tested their first hydrogen bombs. Following these first tests, the two nuclear superpowers worked to develop more hydrogen bombs. These inventions changed the world. For the first time in history, humankind had the power to destroy nearly all life on earth. Khrushchev and Eisenhower were the first leaders to have this military power at their command.

CRACKS IN THE EASTERN BLOC

After Stalin's death, thousands of Soviet political prisoners were released. The

The Warsaw Pact

In May 1955, the Allied occupation of West Germany officially ended. West Germany was allowed to create its own army and to become a member of NATO. Soviet leaders felt threatened by an independent and armed West Germany. In response, the Soviet Union and the Eastern Bloc countries signed the Warsaw Pact on May 14, 1955.

Like the North Atlantic Treaty, the Warsaw Pact tried to create safety by bringing together a large group of nations. But unlike NATO, only one country controlled the alliance—the Soviet Union.

Soviet government turned to producing more consumer goods, such as clothes and furniture, to try to raise the country's standard of living.

In February 1956, Khrushchev made a speech that shocked many Soviet leaders. For six hours, he spoke out against Stalin and his murderous rule. Western leaders were encouraged by Khrushchev's speech. They saw in it hope for a new, less threatening Soviet Union. But Khrushchev's statements angered some Soviet leaders. They believed that Stalin's strength had made the Soviet Union a superpower. They believed the Soviet Union needed to remain strong to remain a world leader. Any sign of weakness might make the Soviet Union and the Eastern Bloc unstable.

By relaxing his grip on power, Khrushchev seemed to be inviting dissent. For example, a few months later, thousands of Poles began protesting against the Polish Communist government. Soviet troops and tanks were called in to maintain control.

Later that year, an even bigger and more violent uprising occurred in Hungary. On October 24, 1956, students held a demonstration (mass gathering) in Budapest, the nation's capital. They wanted reforms, or changes to the government. The government's secret police force fired into the crowds, killing some demonstrators. Groups of Hungarian workers joined the students. The growing mob tore down a statue of Stalin that had stood in the center of the city.

Joyous Hungarians smash a statue of Stalin in Budapest in October 1956. Khrushchev's speech against Stalin let loose a wave of dissent throughout the Eastern Bloc.

As the situation grew more violent, Hungarian Communist leaders called on the Soviet Union for help. During the night, Soviet troops and tanks entered Budapest. The demonstrators fought with the Soviets. Martial law was declared, putting the city under the control of the army.

The Soviets approved a new Hungarian as the Communist leader, Imre Nagy. Nagy was popular among Hungarians. The Soviets believed the Hungarian people would accept Nagy as their leader. The Soviets also believed that Nagy would remain loyal to Soviet leadership. On October 28, Soviet forces pulled out of Budapest.

But the desire for change in Hungary was powerful. Throughout the country, citizens took control of government factories and began to hold elections for a new government. Instead of trying to stop these moves against Soviet leadership, Nagy went along with them. He announced a new government. He also declared Hungary to be neutral—no longer under Soviet control.

Khrushchev had his limits. To allow the Hungarians their freedom, he felt, would

The U-2 Incident

By the late 1950s, the United States had built a "spy plane," an airplane that could fly over the Soviet Union to photograph military sites. The U-2, as the aircraft was called, flew at a very high altitude of more than 80,000 feet—twice as high as most modern airliners fly. U.S. military leaders believed the U-2 flew too high to be shot down by Soviet aircraft and missiles.

But on May 1, 1960, a Soviet missile shot down a U-2 aircraft flying over the Soviet Union. Khrushchev protested to Eisenhower about the invasion of Soviet airspace. Eisenhower denied that the plane had been spying on the Soviet Union. He claimed the aircraft had flown off course while gathering weather information. Eisenhower believed the Soviets had no proof that the plane was a spy plane. Eisenhower had been told the pilot had been killed and the plane destroyed. But the plane's pilot, Gary Francis Powers, had parachuted safely and been taken prisoner by the Soviets. Soviet television broadcast the captured Powers—as well as the U-2's spy cameras—around the world. Eisenhower had lied.

Khrushchev demanded an apology, but Eisenhower refused to offer one. After the incident, Khrushchev canceled a scheduled meeting between the two leaders.

Gary Francis Powers was sentenced to 10 years in a Soviet prison. In 1962 he was exchanged for a Soviet spy captured by the United States.

CIA officials believed that U-2s flew too high to be shot down by Soviet aircraft or missiles. They did not know that the Soviets had worked to build a missile that could knock out the high-flying planes.

be inviting all the Eastern Bloc countries to revolt against the Soviets. Khrushchev reacted swiftly and brutally. On November 4, 1956, Soviet troops and tanks moved into Budapest. For two weeks, Hungarian citizens battled with the Soviet army.

Hungarians made pleas to the West for help. But the United States and its allies did not step in. They expressed sympathy, but the Western powers were not willing to risk a third world war. In the end, the Soviets crushed the Hungarian rebellion. Thousands died on both sides. About 200,000 Hungarians fled to the West. Imre Nagy was executed.

The rise of Khrushchev had brought the world some hope for more freedom in the Soviet Union and Eastern Europe. But the events in Hungary dashed most of these hopes.

THE BERLIN WALL

By the early 1960s, the differences between Communism and Western democracy could be measured in the two Germanys. West Germany had quickly rebuilt itself after the war. The country's citizens were thriving under a capitalist and democratic government. West German factories produced products that were sold throughout the world. The country's workers earned good wages and enjoyed one of the highest standards of living in the world.

East Germany, living under Communist rule, was far less successful. While East Germans received a good education and free health care, they earned low wages and consumer goods were scarce. East Germans also enjoyed far less freedom than their Western neighbors. East

Germany was a totalitarian society. The Stasi, the government's secret police force, spied on the East German population. Thousands of East Germans were jailed as enemies of the Communist government.

Throughout the 1950s, more and more East Germans grew unhappy with life under Communist rule. Thousands illegally left the country, using West Berlin as a gateway, crossing the open border from East Berlin to West Berlin. Between 1949 and 1961, nearly three million East Germans had gone over to the West. This mass exodus, or movement, was draining East Germany.

On August 13, 1961, Soviet and East German officials put a stop to the exodus. East German workers began building a barbed wire fence around West Berlin. By August 15, West Berlin was completely closed off from East Berlin and East Germany. Soon the East German authorities had replaced the barbed wire with concrete walls. Towers with machine guns were added to the structure. Anyone trying

Children stand behind the barbed wire fence that closed off West Berlin from East Berlin.

to cross the wall would be shot on sight.

The Berlin Wall, as it came to be known, became a symbol of a divided world. The wall's barbed wire and machine gun towers symbolized the hatred and distrust between East and West. For Berliners, the wall was an ugly reminder of their city's position at the center of the Cold War.

The Berlin Wall

The Berlin Wall was 11 feet tall or taller in most spots. The structure included watchtowers, guard dogs, and a trench. The trench was dug to keep cars or trucks from gaining enough speed to break through the wall. The wall had three crossing points into and out of East Berlin. They became known as Checkpoint Alpha, Checkpoint Bravo, and Checkpoint Charlie.

Some East Germans still tried to cross into West Berlin. Some climbed the walls. By doing this, they risked being shot and killed by East German border guards. Others dug tunnels underneath the wall. A few tried to fly over in handmade gliders. Some Easterners managed to make a successful run to freedom. Many others died trying.

Berlin Wall

—— Berlin Wall (28.5 miles)
---- "Country Wall (75 miles)

French Sector

West Berlin

British Sector

U.S. Sector

East Berlin

Miles
0 1 2 3 4 5
0 2 4 6
Kilometers

A West Berliner walks along the Berlin Wall. Hundreds of East Germans died trying to cross into West Berlin.

DEMOCRATIC—
5 OR ANTI-COMMUNIST?

While the United States worked to contain Communism, it did not always support freedom and democracy to achieve its goals. During the Cold War, the United States often supported undemocratic and corrupt governments.

Often U.S. leaders backed these governments because they were anti-Communist. Some U.S. officials felt that even a bad government was better than a Communist government. Sometimes U.S. leaders supported corrupt regimes (governments) because they helped U.S. businesses. Citizens living in such countries often resented the United States. They blamed the United States for helping their corrupt and undemocratic government to remain in power.

COMMUNISM IN AMERICA'S BACKYARD

In the late 1950s, the United States' policy of supporting corrupt governments helped set the stage for a Communist revolution very close to its own territory. This occurred in Cuba, the small island nation located just 90 miles off the coast of Florida.

Cuba's unpopular dictator, Fulgencio Batista, was corrupt and undemocratic. Yet the United States had large business investments in Cuba, which Batista protected, so the U.S. government supported the dictator. Most Cubans resented Batista.

In the mid-1950s, a young Cuban lawyer named Fidel Castro formed a rebel group that waged guerrilla warfare against

Batista's government. This kind of fighting involved short surprise attacks on government forces and government buildings. To the people of Cuba, Castro was a freedom fighter, someone who was standing up to Batista's corrupt regime. Most Cubans supported Castro and his guerrillas. On January 1, 1959, Batista fled the country. A week later, Castro marched into Havana, the capital, and took control of Cuba.

President Eisenhower and his staff knew little about Castro. But when Castro's forces executed more than 500 people who had worked with Batista, Americans were alarmed. Thousands of Cubans fled the country. Many moved to the United States to live in exile (outside their homeland).

In 1960 Castro took control of all U.S. businesses in Cuba, making them the property of the government. That same year, Castro looked to the Soviet Union for financial and military aid. Fidel Castro was turning Cuba into a Communist state.

In response, the U.S. government ordered an economic embargo of Cuba. This embargo banned U.S. companies from doing business with the island nation. In January 1961, President Eisenhower broke off relations with Cuba. Fidel Castro's Cuba was an enemy of the United States.

THE BAY OF PIGS INVASION

Meanwhile, U.S. leaders had been working on a plan to remove Castro from power. The

> ### EYEWITNESS QUOTE: INVADING CUBA?
>
> **" There will not be, under any conditions, any intervention in Cuba by United States armed forces."**
>
> —U.S president John F. Kennedy, speaking four days before the Bay of Pigs invasion

CIA began training a group of Cuban exiles to invade Cuba. The small anti-Castro army planned to secretly land on the island and create a new revolution. They would overthrow Castro's government and replace it with a U.S.-friendly regime. In April 1961, the new U.S. president, John F. Kennedy, approved the invasion plan. But he kept the United States' role a secret. Kennedy believed that trying to overthrow another government would make the United States look bad in the eyes of the world.

On April 17, about 1,300 exiles, armed with American weapons, landed at the Bahía de Cochinos (Bay of Pigs) on Cuba's southern coast. They hoped to win the support of the local Cubans. Instead, Castro's army crushed them. More than 100 of the invaders were killed by Castro's troops. Only 14 escaped. The rest were taken prisoner.

Cuban forces captured most of the Bay of Pigs invaders. Castro exchanged the prisoners for millions of dollars' worth of U.S. food and medicine in December 1962.

The Bay of Pigs invasion was a humiliating disaster. The world quickly realized that the United States had been behind the invasion. The U.S. government looked foolish, weak, and dishonest to the world. With the United States as his proven enemy, Castro asked for more financial and military support from the Soviet Union.

THE CUBAN MISSILE CRISIS

Soviet premier Khrushchev wanted Cuba as an ally, because it would provide a Soviet missile base close to the United States. In the early 1960s, the United States had missiles stationed in Turkey, near the Soviet border. These U.S. missiles had the power to quickly strike the USSR. The Soviets had no missile bases close to the United States. If the United States struck first in a nuclear war, it might have been able to wipe out the USSR before it could strike back.

But a base in Cuba would eliminate the advantage the United States had in Turkey. And Soviet missiles would also protect Castro from another U.S. invasion. In the summer of 1962, the Soviet Union began to secretly install missiles and their launchers in Cuba.

A few months later, on October 14, a U.S. U-2 spy plane took pictures of the

This and other U-2 photos, showing Soviet missile bases being built on Cuba, launched the Cuban Missile Crisis. The events that followed brought the world to the brink of nuclear war.

missile bases. Early the next morning, President Kennedy learned about the missiles. He and his staff decided that the missiles had to be removed or destroyed. They debated how to handle the situation. Bomb the sites? Invade Cuba, remove Castro, and destroy the missile sites? Some U.S. leaders supported such a tough response. But others feared that such an attack might lead to a Soviet nuclear counterattack. What if an attack on Cuba started World War III? These people advised Kennedy to find a different solution.

Kennedy did not want to be responsible for starting a nuclear war. So he chose a firm, but nonviolent route. On October 22, he appeared on television and told the American public about the Cuban missiles. Kennedy demanded that the Soviets remove all of their weapons from Cuba. The president ordered a military quarantine, or blockade, around Cuba. U.S. Navy ships would surround the island and keep the Soviet Union from sending in more weapons. He announced that the United States would consider any nuclear missile launched from Cuba as an attack on the United States by the Soviet Union. That would lead to a counterattack on the Soviet Union. Kennedy added, "I call upon Chairman Khrushchev to halt and eliminate this . . . threat to world peace. . . ."

The U.S. military went on full alert. U.S. bombers circled the skies outside of Soviet airspace. They were ready to attack at a moment's notice.

John F. Kennedy

U.S. submarines, equipped with missiles carrying nuclear warheads, patrolled the seas off the Soviet coast. In the United States, military units prepared for a possible invasion of Cuba.

The American public was on full alert too. Many feared that a full-scale nuclear war was about to begin. For the next few days, Americans woke up each morning wondering if it might be their last day on earth—or the last day *for* earth.

Meanwhile, in Cuba, Soviet commanders in charge of the missile sites were on high alert too. They had been ordered to use nuclear weapons if U.S. forces invaded the island.

On October 26, Khrushchev sent Kennedy a letter in which he offered an exchange. He would remove Soviet missiles and military personnel (persons) from Cuba if the United States guaranteed it would not invade the island.

Kennedy and his advisers considered this offer. But before they had a chance to reply, Khrushchev sent a second letter, demanding that the United States remove its missiles from Turkey. Then, he said, the Soviet Union would remove its missiles from Cuba.

Robert F. Kennedy, the president's brother and the U. S. attorney general, suggested that Kennedy ignore

EYEWITNESS QUOTE:
THE CUBAN MISSILE CRISIS

"We and you ought not to pull on the end of the rope in which we have tied the knot of war, because the more we pull the tighter the knot will be tied."

—letter to U.S. president John F. Kennedy from Soviet premier Nikita Khrushchev

Khrushchev's second letter. So the president publicly announced that he would accept the offer made in Khrushchev's first letter. The U.S. invasion of Cuba was called off. The world breathed a sigh of relief. Nuclear war had been avoided.

A SECRET DEAL

Unknown to the public, President Kennedy and Premier Khrushchev had made a second agreement. The United States would secretly remove its missiles from Turkey. This agreement was kept confidential because the American public might have protested against bargaining with the Soviets. In exchange, on October 28, Khrushchev announced that the Soviets were removing the Cuban missile bases and returning them to the Soviet

> ### EYEWITNESS QUOTE: THE CUBAN MISSILE CRISIS
>
> " It was a beautiful fall evening, the height of the crisis, and I went up into the open air to look and to smell it, because I thought it was the last Saturday I would ever see."
>
> —U.S. secretary of defense **Robert M. McNamara**

Union. He also announced that he trusted the United States not to invade Cuba.

Although the United States had gotten the Soviet missiles removed from Cuba, Khrushchev could still call the crisis a victory. He had succeeded in getting rid of the U.S. missiles in Turkey. Other Soviet officials saw the Cuban Missile Crisis as a defeat. They felt Khrushchev had shown weakness by agreeing to remove the weapons from Cuba.

By keeping the Turkish missile plan a secret, Kennedy claimed victory. Americans believed that Kennedy had forced the Soviet Union to remove the Cuban missiles. Perhaps the biggest winner of all had been the world as a whole. It had avoided a devastating nuclear war.

Khrushchev *(right)* and Kennedy *(left)* worked out a secret deal to end the Cuban Missile Crisis. Following the crisis, both leaders made an effort toward better relations.

A THAW IN THE COLD WAR

Following the Cuban Missile Crisis, Kennedy and Khrushchev worked toward friendlier relations. Neither leader wanted to trigger such a frightening showdown again. In July 1963, the United States, the Soviet Union, and Great Britain signed a nuclear test ban treaty. To protect the environment, each of the countries agreed to stop testing nuclear weapons above ground. In the future, the three countries would conduct all nuclear tests in underground tunnels. President Kennedy explained the importance of the agreement in a statement to the American public: "For the first time an agreement has been reached on bringing the forces of nuclear destruction under international control. . . . " The test ban treaty was the beginning of a trend to control the spread of nuclear weapons.

Kennedy and Khrushchev set up a telephone hotline. The hotline directly connected a special phone in the president's office in Washington, D.C., to a phone in the Soviet premier's office in Moscow. The Cuban Missile Crisis had shown both leaders that a disagreement between the two countries could be a threat to the whole world. By improving communication, U.S. and Soviet leaders had a better chance of talking through problems instead of going to war.

The thaw (improvement) in U.S.-Soviet relations continued. In 1963 the Soviet Union faced a dangerous shortage of grain. Many citizens were threatened with starvation. President Kennedy agreed to a plan to sell millions of dollars' worth of American wheat to the Soviet Union. Some saw the agreement as a friendly gesture by the United States.

Many Soviets considered it a humiliating defeat. They felt that asking the enemy for food was a sign of weakness.

Within two years of the Cuban Missile Crisis, both leaders were gone from the world stage. In November 1963, John F. Kennedy was assassinated in Dallas, Texas. Less than a year later, Soviet Communist officials staged a coup (overthrow). Khrushchev was forced to retire.

Khrushchev had become unpopular. The Soviet economy was in trouble and the nation's standard of living was still very low. Many Soviets were angered about their nation's defeat during the Cuban Missile Crisis.

Leonid Brezhnev and Alexei Kosygin became the USSR's top leaders. Vice President Lyndon B. Johnson replaced Kennedy as president. These men faced major challenges in their new roles.

The End of Khrushchev's Rule

Soviet leaders blamed Khrushchev for the country's grain shortage in the early 1960s. The problem had been partly the result of Khrushchev's agricultural plans. In an attempt to increase the Soviet Union's farming production, he had made changes to the nation's farming methods. These changes included trying to plant crops in areas where the soil and climate would not support them. These changes were disastrous and led to the embarrassing purchase of wheat from the United States. The episode gave the anti-Khrushchev Soviets another reason to remove him from power.

THE SPACE RACE

Beginning in the late 1950s, the United States and the Soviet Union raced to outdo one another in space exploration and space travel. The "space race," as it was called, was a competition to show which country had the best technology.

The Soviets fired the opening shot of this Cold War battle. On October 4, 1957, Soviet scientists launched *Sputnik I*, the first man-made satellite to orbit, or circle, the earth. *Sputnik I*, which means "fellow traveler" in Russian, broadcast a series of radio beeps back to earth. After *Sputnik I*, U.S. scientists rushed to launch their own satellite. On January 31, 1958, the United States sent *Explorer I* into orbit. That same year, the U.S. government formed the National Aeronautics and Space Administration (NASA) to run the country's space program.

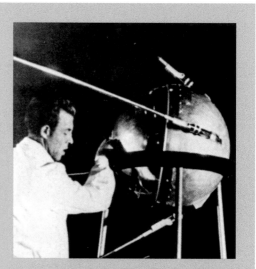

The Soviet satellite *Sputnik I* was about 22 inches in diameter and weighed about 184 pounds.

The Soviet lead in the space race sent the United States into a panic. To the American public, it appeared the Soviets had passed the United States in technology and education. According to historian Norman Friedman, "Much was made of how many more Soviet than U.S. citizens were [studying the] sciences." The U.S. government responded by making science a much more important subject in schools.

On April 12, 1961, Yuri Gagarin of the Soviet Union became the world's first cosmonaut—the Russian term for astronaut—when he completed one orbit of the earth aboard *Vostok*. Citizens celebrated in the streets throughout the Soviet Union, and Gagarin became a

Soviet cosmonaut Yuri Gagarin's successful orbit of earth caused a sensation in the United States. Many Americans feared losing the space race.

national hero. Not until nearly a year later did John Glenn become the first American to orbit the earth, circling the globe three times.

Early in 1961, President Kennedy declared that the United States would, "before the decade is out . . . land a man on the moon and return him safely to earth." The race to the moon was on, and both superpowers would spend billions on the race to get there.

The Soviets scored another first in March 1965, when cosmonaut Alexei A. Leonov became the first man to walk in space. Three months later, U.S. astronaut Edward H. White II made the first American space walk.

The United States took the lead in the space race a year later, when two NASA space vehicles successfully linked up while in orbit. Late in 1968, NASA scored another first, when *Apollo 8* became the first manned space vehicle to orbit the moon.

The following summer, on July 16, 1969, *Apollo 11* blasted off from Cape Canaveral, Florida, on its way to the moon. Billions of people around the world followed the journey of Apollo 11 on television. Four days later, on July 20, the spacecraft's lunar module—the vehicle designed to land on the moon—touched down on the moon. A short time later, as the world watched on television, astronaut Neil Armstrong became the first person to set foot on the moon.

The moon landing was the United States' biggest space race victory. To Americans, it showed that U.S. technology had taken the lead again. Meanwhile, the Soviet government claimed that it had had no interest in landing on the moon. Decades later, these claims were proven false. In fact, the Soviets had tried to build a lunar landing craft. But the program had failed and had been kept a secret.

U.S. astronaut Buzz Aldrin on the surface of the moon, July 1969. The photo was taken by his fellow moonwalker, Neil Armstrong.

VIETNAM AND
6 THE PRAGUE SPRING

President Kennedy's assassination shocked the world. But the young president's violent death was one of many explosive events of the 1960s. In the United States, the 1960s was a period of intense change.

When Lyndon B. Johnson took the oath of office, moments after President Kennedy's death, he promised to tackle many tough issues. The civil rights movement was active, as millions of African Americans banded together to demand their equal rights in American society. The women's rights movement was active too, with women fighting for equal pay for equal work and other rights. But Johnson was also taking on

a growing conflict in Southeast Asia, in the nation of Vietnam.

COMMUNISM IN SOUTHEAST ASIA

The conflict in Vietnam had its roots even before World War II. France had ruled the country for many years before the war. But the Japanese forced the French out of part of the country during World War II. Vietnamese citizens, including Vietnamese Communists, resisted both French and Japanese rule. The Vietnamese Communists, under their leader Ho Chi Minh, received support from the United States. In return for helping in the fight against the

Ho Chi Minh

Japanese, Ho hoped the United States would support Vietnamese independence. But after the war, the French wanted to rule all of Vietnam. The United States stayed out of the conflict between the French and the Vietnamese Communists.

Beginning in 1945, the French and the Vietnamese Communists fought a long and bloody war. Although the French had well-trained soldiers and better equipment, they could not defeat the Communists.

Ho Chi Minh's forces, known as the Viet Minh, received supplies from China and the Soviet Union. The Viet Minh used guerrilla tactics. They made surprise attacks on French forces and then slipped away. The Viet Minh hid in Vietnam's dense jungles, where the French could not easily find them.

The Viet Minh's style of fighting was costly for both sides. By the mid-1950s, the French began looking for a way out of the long, costly war. Meanwhile, the United States was becoming more interested in Vietnam. U.S. leaders did not want to see a Communist government leading the country.

During this period, U.S. president Eisenhower and his staff came up with the term "domino theory." They believed that if one Southeast Asian country fell to the Communists, others would too. Each would topple one after another, just like dominoes. The entire region of Southeast Asia under the influence of the USSR and China would be a threat to the West. Eisenhower did not want Vietnam to be the first domino.

In July 1954, the French and the Vietnamese Communists signed an agreement in Geneva, dividing Vietnam into northern and southern regions. Ho Chi Minh ruled a Communist government in North Vietnam. Ngo Dinh Diem led South Vietnam's anti-Communist government. The United States supported Diem's government with financial aid and weapons.

The Geneva Agreement was supposed to end all fighting in Vietnam. Elections were planned to reunify the country under a single government. But a nationwide election never occurred, and fighting between the North and the South continued.

The United States supported South Vietnamese president Ngo Dinh Diem because of his tough stance against Communism. But Diem's brutal rule made him unpopular in his home country.

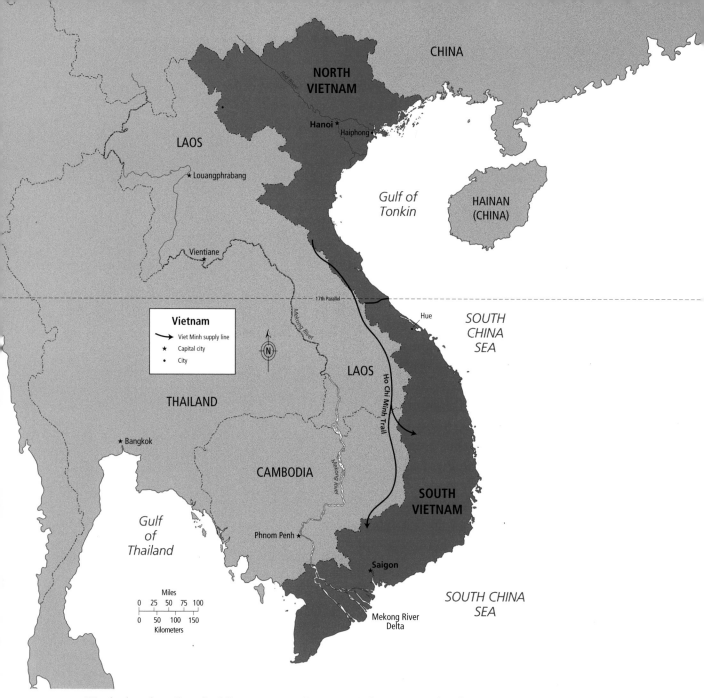

To help the South Vietnamese, President Eisenhower began sending military advisers to the country. These men trained South Vietnamese soldiers and helped South Vietnamese military leaders plan war strategy. When Kennedy became president, he sent more advisers.

But the American advisers had a difficult job helping Diem. The South Vietnamese leader was very unpopular. He tortured, imprisoned, and executed many people who resisted his rule. Many South Vietnamese chose to fight against him.

These people formed a group known as the National Liberation Front (NLF) of South Vietnam. They called for the overthrow of Diem. The North Vietnamese Communists supported the NLF with weapons and supplies. The NLF staged terrorist attacks. They bombed buildings and murdered Diem supporters. In response, Diem ordered attacks on suspected NLF hideouts. Over the next few years, the conflict in Vietnam grew more and more violent.

By 1963 approximately 16,000 American military advisers were in Vietnam. American leaders had come to see that Diem and his corrupt leadership would not be able to defeat the Communists. They encouraged South Vietnamese military officers to stage a coup to overthrow Diem. On November 1, 1963, these officers overthrew Diem's government. Diem was murdered. Three weeks later, Kennedy himself was murdered and President Johnson took over the mess in Vietnam.

THE VIETNAM WAR

By early 1964, the NLF had gained control of large areas of South Vietnam. Meanwhile, the North Vietnamese began

EYEWITNESS QUOTE:
THE VIETNAM WAR

"I am not going to lose Vietnam. I am not going to be the President who saw Southeast Asia go the way of China."

— U.S. president Lyndon B. Johnson

sending soldiers south to fight alongside the NLF.

President Johnson decided to take more forceful steps. In early 1965, he ordered a series of air strikes against North Vietnamese targets. American aircraft attacked North Vietnamese bases, factories, and supply lines.

With the air strikes, the first American combat troops arrived in Vietnam to protect the U.S. air bases in South Vietnam. At this point, most Americans believed that the U.S. mission to contain Communism in Vietnam was the right thing to do.

American military commanders quickly learned what the French had discovered years earlier—the Vietnamese Communists were a tough enemy. The U.S. air strikes seemed to have little effect, and Communist attacks increased throughout South Vietnam. President Johnson sent more U.S. soldiers. By the spring of 1965, 70,000 American service personnel were in Vietnam.

Lyndon Baines Johnson

Lyndon Baines Johnson was born on August 27, 1908, in central Texas. He served in the U.S. Navy during World War II. In 1948 Johnson was elected to the U.S. Senate and ran as John F. Kennedy's vice president in the 1960 presidential election. Johnson became president when Kennedy was killed in 1963. The big, likable, and outgoing LBJ, as he was often called, was a popular figure with the American public in the early years of his presidency.

Under enemy fire, U.S. troops sprint through a South Vietnamese city during the Vietnam War. As the war dragged on and a growing number of U.S. soldiers died, more Americans began to question and criticize the war.

The war continued to grow. By early 1967, 400,000 U.S. soldiers were in Vietnam. Although U.S. and South Vietnamese forces won every major battle, the Communists refused to stop fighting.

Like the Korean War, the conflict in Vietnam was a limited war. President Johnson did not want to bring the Chinese or the Soviets into the conflict. Instead, U.S. forces tried to cause enough damage to force the Communists to negotiate for peace.

Meanwhile, thousands of Americans and tens of thousands of Vietnamese were dying in the war. Millions of Americans began to wonder if it was right for the United States to wage war on another country because of its political system. They also protested against the draft,

which required young American men to serve in the military. The draft was forcing many to join the army to fight a war they didn't believe in. Thousands began gathering in demonstrations to protest the war in Vietnam.

Yet many Americans supported the war. They believed that Communism was a serious threat to America and the world. They also pointed out that the United States had promised to protect South Vietnam from Communism. To back out would be a terrible sign of weakness and might encourage Communism in other parts of the world. The Vietnam War threatened to tear the country apart.

On March 31, 1968, Johnson announced he would not run for reelection later that year. A new president—Richard M. Nixon—

was left with the painful task of ending the Vietnam War.

THE PRAGUE SPRING

Meanwhile, the Soviet Union was experiencing its own challenges. In the late 1960s, the standard of living grew worse for many people in the Eastern Bloc. Some of the Communist governments tried to make changes to improve their economic situation. For example, in Prague, the capital of Czechoslovakia, the government gave the media more freedom. Citizens and leaders had new freedom to discuss the country's troubles and to debate ways to solve them. Many Czechs began openly criticizing the government, the Soviet Union, and Communism. A new spirit of freedom swept through the country. This rebirth came to be known as the Prague Spring.

Soviet and Warsaw Pact leaders considered the new spirit of freedom dangerous. They feared that Czechoslovakia's changes would lead to a loss of Soviet control, that citizens of other Warsaw Pact nations might start calling for similar reforms. By mid-1968, nearly all Warsaw Pact leaders had spoken out against the Czech reforms.

To bring an end to the Prague Spring, the Soviets invaded Czechoslovakia—just as they had done years before in Hungary.

Only this time, armed forces from other Warsaw Pact nations joined the Soviet tanks and troops. On August 20, 1968, half a million Warsaw Pact troops poured into Czechoslovakia. The Czechs were quickly overwhelmed. The Czech leaders of reform were replaced and sent into exile. Once again, the Soviet Union had used armed force to maintain control.

Warsaw Pact tanks and troops invaded Czechoslovakia to crush the Prague Spring. Completely overwhelmed, Czech citizens quickly abandoned their hopes for freedom and democracy.

MINORITIES DURING THE COLD WAR

Many Americans saw the Cold War as a struggle of American freedom and justice against Soviet oppression, or unfair use of power. Yet a large percentage of Americans did not have freedom and justice at home. African Americans and other American minority groups—Latinos, Asians, Native Americans, and others—often did not enjoy equal rights or equal treatment. Segregation laws forced minorities to live, work, eat, and shop separately from whites. Most American minorities were poor. And racial hatred at times led to the murder of minorities by angry whites.

In the 1920s, the American Communist Party attracted minority members by criticizing the unfair treatment of minorities. One African American described why he supported the Communist Party: "I've never known a Communist . . . to mob a man outside city hall, lynch [hang] him . . . and everything else, even shoot him on sight." In fact, lawyers from the American Communist Party often defended minorities in criminal cases.

Jamaican-born poet and short story writer Claude McKay was a prominent Communist during New York City's Harlem Renaissance of the 1920s. His works, written both in Harlem and during travels in Europe, include *Harlem Shadows*, *Home to Harlem*, and *Banjo*.

The Cold War changed some U.S. leaders' attitudes toward racial problems in the United States. In the decade following World War II, many countries in Africa were achieving independence. Some U.S. officials feared that the unfair treatment of blacks in the United States would lead these African countries to side with the Soviet Union. These fears led some U.S. leaders to support civil rights for minorities. The civil rights movement, under the leadership of Dr. Martin Luther King, gained many supporters during the 1950s.

Yet other white leaders fought against the civil rights movement. These men—including FBI director J. Edgar Hoover—accused the movement of having Communist ties. The FBI often harassed King and other civil rights leaders by spying on them and recording their conversations.

Despite these problems, the civil rights movement achieved a major victory in 1964. On July 2, President Lyndon B. Johnson signed the Civil Rights Act of 1964. The act made segregation in schools, restaurants, hotels, parks, and other public places illegal. The act was a first step toward ending injustices against minorities in the United States. This act and other civil rights acts that followed, helped the United States to become a more fair and just country.

WOMEN DURING THE COLD WAR

You'll be happier with a HOOVER

Soviet women usually could not buy the household appliances American women enjoyed.

American and Soviet women led very different lives during the Cold War years. American women were expected to give up the jobs they had held during World War II to become full-time homemakers and mothers. The economic boom of the 1950s allowed American women to purchase new and better "labor-saving" products, such as vacuum cleaners and washing machines.

By the 1960s, a growing number of American women were choosing to work outside of the home. Yet American society often discouraged such changes, believing that a woman's place was in the home. At the same time, American women rarely received equal pay for equal work and had few opportunities for high-level jobs. In response to these pressures, movements calling for women's rights gathered strength.

The American women's rights movement had an impact on the Cold War. In the late 1960s, many of the same women who called for equal rights for women also marched against the Vietnam War and protested against the proliferation of nuclear weapons.

During the Cold War years, Soviet women also held the responsibility of raising children and taking care of their homes and families. But these duties had to be performed in addition to working full-time outside of the home. Nearly all Soviet women were expected to work, often in difficult, dirty, and dangerous jobs, and usually for far less pay than men earned.

Soviet women enjoyed few of the luxuries that American women had. Consumer goods remained scarce in the Soviet Union throughout the Cold War years, and labor-saving devices were usually rare or impossible to find. Citizens were often forced to stand in line for hours—sometimes days or even weeks—to purchase goods. In most cases, women were the ones expected to do the waiting. According to one Soviet writer: "A typical Soviet woman holds down three jobs at once: the one for which she gets money; then the job of standing in endless lines and dragging home shopping bags of food; and finally the care of the children, the home, and particularly the kitchen."

By the 1960s, as American women called for more access to the workplace, many Soviet women were wearing down from overwork. But as the Communist system continued to struggle during the Cold War years, women would still be needed in the Soviet workforce, and the lives of most Soviet women would remain a struggle.

DÉTENTE

7

In the late 1960s, the United States and the USSR were spending huge amounts of money to maintain a balance of power. Both sides knew that the arms race could not go on forever. Even if a nuclear war never took place, the cost of producing so many weapons was a drain on the economies of both superpowers. So the United States and the Soviet Union began working toward détente. *Détente* is a French term that refers to the relaxation of strained relationships.

LIMITING NUCLEAR WEAPONS

Both nations were worried about the proliferation, or spread, of nuclear weapons to other countries. Great Britain and France had developed nuclear weapons in the years following World War II. China exploded its first atomic bomb in 1964. So on July 1, 1968, the Soviet Union, the United States, and many other nations signed the Nuclear Non-Proliferation Treaty (NPT).

The treaty's goal was to strictly control the spread of nuclear weapons. Signatories (signers of the treaty) whose nations had nuclear weapons agreed not to help other nations develop them. These nations also agreed to help nonnuclear nations develop peaceful uses of nuclear power, such as the building of nuclear power plants to generate electricity. All countries with nuclear weapons also agreed to work toward nuclear disarmament (to get rid of their nuclear weapons).

Signatories that did not have nuclear weapons agreed not to develop or acquire them. They also agreed to allow their countries' peaceful nuclear programs to be supervised by a new UN agency, the International Atomic Energy Agency.

STRATEGIC ARMS LIMITATION TALKS

On the day the NPT was signed, the United States and the USSR announced they would begin negotiations for limiting their huge nuclear arsenals (supplies of weapons). Both nations had thousands of nuclear weapons—more than enough to destroy one another and the world with them. And each side continued to build better weapons, replacing old ones with more sophisticated systems. The arms race had become extremely expensive for both countries. The negotiations, called the Strategic Arms Limitation Talks (SALT), were meant to reduce military spending by putting a freeze on the number of weapons each nation could own.

The first round of SALT meetings took place between 1969 and 1972 and led to two major agreements. The first agreement strictly limited the building of antiballistic missiles (ABMs—missiles built to shoot down other missiles). The second agreement called for a freeze on the number of missiles in each nation's stockpile (supply). The agreements were part of the Strategic Arms Limitation Treaty, which was signed on May 26, 1972.

SALT was praised as an encouraging sign of détente. It showed that the two superpowers were trying to cooperate to make the world a safer place. But SALT had more to do with economics than with safety. ABMs were extremely expensive. They were also unreliable. Scientists did not know if they would really work in a nuclear attack. Limiting their proliferation would save billions of dollars on both sides.

ABMs, like the two shown launching here, have never been proven to be effective.

THE ARMS RACE

By the late 1950s, both the United States and the Soviet Union had built enough nuclear bombs to completely destroy one another—and possibly the whole world with them. While both superpowers tried to avoid such a war, they also spent huge amounts of money trying to build weapons that could win a nuclear battle. The idea was to wipe out the enemy before it could strike back. So hitting first was the key to winning.

But the process of building missiles is complicated and expensive. Both the United States and the Soviet Union spent billions of dollars on missiles. They built intercontinental ballistic missiles (ICBMs). ICBMs could travel thousands of miles to strike a distant continent.

By the mid-1960s, both countries had built hundreds of ICBMs. Yet each nation kept building more powerful missiles that could be launched as quickly as possible. The United States and the Soviet Union also created huge stockpiles of nuclear warheads—the part of the missile that held the nuclear explosive.

Once ICBMs had been built, the two countries tried to find ways to shoot down missiles. Antiballistic missiles (ABMs) were designed to knock missiles out before they could reach their targets. But ABMs were very expensive, and they often did not work. Destroying a missile that is flying several thousand miles an hour is very hard to do.

A Minuteman III missile armed with an MIRV nuclear warhead rests in a silo.

Still, American scientists created missiles that worked against ABMs. These multiple independently targetable reentry vehicles (MIRVs) carry several warheads in a single ICBM. Once the ICBM is over enemy territory, the MIRV splits up. Each warhead hits a different target. The MIRV made the ABM's job almost impossible. A fleet of ABMs might be able to destroy some MIRVs, but not all of them. Once the Soviets realized that the Americans were creating MIRVs, they rushed to build their own.

By the late 1960s, both superpowers were looking for a way to slow down the arms race. Each country knew that no one could hold the lead for long. Every time one superpower built a new kind of missile, the other superpower quickly built its own version. The huge costs of missile development and production were hurting their economies.

Richard M. Nixon

"VIETNAMIZATION"

As the SALT talks were beginning, Richard M. Nixon became president of the United States. He promised to end the Vietnam War, bringing "peace with honor." This meant ending the war—or at least ending American involvement in it—without losing to the Communists.

Nixon announced a new approach to the war, "Vietnamization." Its goal was to have the South Vietnamese do more of the fighting against the Vietnamese Communists. U.S. forces would continue to support the South Vietnamese, but American troops would gradually leave Vietnam. Meanwhile, Nixon and his national security adviser, Henry Kissinger, tried to negotiate with the North Vietnamese for a peaceful end to the war.

Then in May 1970, Nixon made a sudden change. He ordered troops to invade Cambodia, Vietnam's neighbor, to destroy Communist bases there. Nixon said that the invasion was to help defeat the Communists, but many Americans were outraged at the action. Protests erupted throughout the country. "Peace with honor" was turning out to be very difficult to achieve.

The Cambodian invasion did not break the Vietnamese Communists. In the spring of 1972, the North Vietnamese launched a huge invasion of the South. Nixon launched massive air strikes against North Vietnam. The fierce bombing convinced the North Vietnamese to negotiate an end to the war.

Late in 1972, Henry Kissinger announced that the United States and North Vietnam had reached a peace agreement. Then the North Vietnamese pulled out of the agreement. Determined to end the war once and for all, Nixon ordered another massive bombing campaign. The air strikes convinced the North Vietnamese to stop fighting. A peace agreement was signed in Paris on January 27, 1973. By the end of March, the last U.S. troops had left Vietnam.

Yet the war did not end there. The peace agreement quickly fell apart. In early 1975, the North Vietnamese launched a massive invasion of the South. Without American firepower to back them up, South Vietnamese forces were overwhelmed. On April 30, 1975, North Vietnamese tanks smashed through the gates of the South Vietnamese presidential palace in Saigon. The South Vietnamese surrendered. The war was finally over. Vietnam was united under Communist rule. The United States had lost a major Cold War battle.

U.S. soldiers wade through swampy waters during the Vietnam War. Some 58,000 Americans died as a result of the war.

DÉTENTE CONTINUED

Shortly before the Vietnam War came to an end, a political scandal forced Nixon to resign as president. Nixon's vice president,

Watergate

Nixon's presidency was ruined by a scandal that came to be known as Watergate. The scandal got its name from the Watergate complex of apartment and office buildings in Washington, D.C. There on June 17, 1972, police arrested five men who had broken into the headquarters of Nixon's opponents in the election, the Democratic National Party. It turned out that the burglars worked for Nixon's reelection committee.

Nixon and his staff denied having any involvement with the break-in. But as more details became public, it became clear that the president and his staff were lying. For the next two years, the Watergate scandal grew. Evidence of illegal activities by Nixon and his staff became public. These activities included spying on Nixon's political opponents and using government agents to harass Nixon's enemies. In late 1973, the U.S. Congress began to take steps to impeach Nixon, or remove him from office. Not wanting to be impeached, Richard M. Nixon resigned in August 1974.

Soviet leaders were amazed by the Watergate scandal. They could not believe that the president of the United States, the most powerful man in the world, had been pushed out of office. Watergate showed the power of democracy and of a free, open media. It showed that a democratic leader had to answer for his or her actions and that a free, open media could challenge the most powerful politician in the country.

Gerald R. Ford, took office. During his short time as president, Ford worked to continue détente. U.S. and Soviet officials worked toward a second SALT treaty, but with no success. President Ford also participated in the Conference on Security and Cooperation in Europe, talks aimed at friendlier relations between the Eastern and Western blocs.

The conference led to the August 1975 Helsinki Accords, signed by 35 nations (the United States, the Soviet Union, the Eastern Bloc nations, and others) in Helsinki, Finland. The agreement called for peaceful settlements of conflicts among European countries. This part of the agreement also brought recognition, or agreement, on Europe's post-World War II borders. In the 30 years since the end of the war, several Western nations had refused to officially recognize the borders of the Eastern Bloc countries. Western governments believed that the Soviet Union had taken control of these nations illegally. The Helsinki Accords brought a close to this long-standing Cold War issue.

Another part of the accords encouraged more ties—such as more trade—between East and West. It also encouraged cultural and educational exchanges and cooperation in scientific and industrial areas.

Soviet leaders considered some of the Helsinki Accords a great victory. The economies of the Eastern Bloc nations were suffering badly under Communism. Industry was far behind the West. The standard of living for most citizens in Communist countries was very poor. Eastern Bloc leaders hoped that more trade with the West would help improve the situation.

U.S. president Gerald R. Ford *(seated, center)* signs the Helsinki Accords in the summer of 1975.

The Soviets were not as enthusiastic about the cultural part of the agreement. This part declared that "the participating States will respect human rights and fundamental freedoms, including the freedom of thought, conscience, religion or belief." But the Western governments insisted on this part of the agreement. Desperate to receive economic benefits, the Communist governments agreed to all the terms of the accords.

Soon after the Helsinki Accords were signed, Western leaders realized that the Communists would not respect freedom and human rights. When Western leaders protested, Brezhnev said, "We are masters in our own house, and we shall decide what we implement and what we ignore." Détente began to unravel.

However, some Eastern Bloc citizens tried to force their governments to live up to the Helsinki Accords. These people started movements in Poland, Czechoslovakia, and other countries in the East. Although they had little success early on, these dissidents (people who challenged their governments) were setting the stage for changes in the future.

The Apollo-Soyuz Test Project

In July 1975, the spirit of détente expanded into outer space when NASA astronauts and Soviet cosmonauts worked together in space for the first time. The Apollo-Soyuz Test Project was designed to see if American and Soviet spacecraft could meet and link in space.

On July 15, the Soviets launched a Soyuz spacecraft from the Soviet Union, while NASA launched an Apollo spacecraft from Cape Canaveral, Florida. Two days later, the world watched on television as the two capsules met and linked in space. The American and Soviet

American astronauts and Soviet cosmonauts send greetings to earth from space. The Apollo-Soyuz Test Project was one of the high points of U.S-Soviet relations during the Cold War.

travelers exchanged warm greetings, and the teams took turns visiting each others' spacecraft. For two days, the teams performed experiments together, such as testing radiation levels in the solar system and testing how living in outer space affects the human body.

The two spacecraft separated on July 19. The spirit of goodwill created by the Apollo-Soyuz Test Project seemed to show that U.S.-Soviet relations were warming up.

Jimmy Carter was inaugurated as president of the United States on January 20, 1977. In his speech, he stated his "ultimate goal, the elimination of all nuclear weapons from earth." To do this, Carter tried to continue détente. But Carter also had strong beliefs about the importance of human rights. Coming to terms with Soviet leaders on both nuclear weapons and human rights was difficult.

Shortly after taking office, Carter proposed that the United States and the Soviet Union both cut back on nuclear weapons. But just before offering the disarmament proposal to the Soviets, Carter publicly praised dissidents in Communist nations. Soviet leaders were offended and rejected the nuclear proposal.

The new president also criticized human rights abuses in the Eastern Bloc. Soviet leaders were offended by these remarks too. "We do not need any teachers when it comes to the internal affairs of our country," said one Soviet official.

Carter's support of human rights led many dissidents to increase their criticism of their governments. They called for the Eastern Bloc governments to honor the Helsinki Accords. But the Communist governments did not listen to these requests. Instead, many dissidents were imprisoned, exiled, or sent to mental institutions.

Although Carter's focus on human rights made arms negotiations difficult, American and Soviet officials continued to work for a new agreement. Carter and Brezhnev signed a new treaty, SALT II, in June 1979. The treaty called for new limits on long-range bombers and missiles. But the U.S. Congress then had to approve SALT II. Events far away from Washington,

Jimmy Carter

James Earl Carter Jr. was born October 1, 1924, in Plains, Georgia. He grew up on a small peanut farm near Plains. An excellent student, Carter studied at the U.S. Naval Academy in Annapolis, Maryland, in the mid-1940s. After graduating, he served in the navy, sailing on the world's first nuclear-powered submarine. He left the navy in 1953 to return to Plains. In 1962 Carter won a seat in the Georgia State Senate.

Elected governor of Georgia in 1970, Carter gained national attention when he spoke out for equal rights for minorities. In 1976 he defeated Gerald Ford in the presidential race and served one term.

D.C., would lead Congress and President Carter to reject SALT II.

AFGHANISTAN

More than a year before the SALT II treaty was signed, a group of military officers staged a coup in the Central Asian nation of Afghanistan. The officers had been trained by the Soviet military. But the Soviets denied having a role in the overthrow.

The new Afghan leaders tried to create a Soviet-style government. But these changes were unpopular among many Afghans, especially Afghan Muslims (followers of Islam). Communism outlawed religious practice.

Afghan mullahs, or Muslim religious leaders, called on Afghan citizens to rise up against the new government. Many Afghan men became mujahideen ("soldiers of God"), forming guerrilla groups that attacked and killed Afghan government officials. They also killed Soviets who were working for the Afghan regime.

Soviet leaders feared more Islamic revolutions would spread to nearby Muslim areas within the Soviet Union, such as Turkmenistan and Tajikistan. They also feared such revolutions might lead other Soviet Bloc nations to try to break away from Soviet control. In December 1979, Soviet troops and tanks invaded Afghanistan to crush the mujahideen.

President Carter was outraged. He and many U.S. leaders feared the Soviets were trying to take over the nearby Persian Gulf area—an oil-rich region that includes Iran, Iraq, and Saudi Arabia. Such a takeover would give the Soviets control of much of the world's oil supply. If the Soviets controlled the Persian Gulf's oil, they would have a stranglehold on the world economy.

Muslim mujahideen (*above*) fought a destructive and bloody war against the invading Soviets. In Afghanistan, the Soviet Union faced many of the same difficulties the United States had faced in Vietnam.

Carter called the Soviet invasion of Afghanistan "the most serious threat to peace since the Second World War." The United States ordered a trade embargo on the Soviet Union. Détente was collapsing.

SUPPORTING THE MUJAHIDEEN

The Soviets removed the new Afghan government from power, killed its leaders, and chose new rulers. But the mujahideen refused to accept the new government. The Muslim fighters began attacking the Soviets.

The Olympic Boycotts

Throughout the Cold War, the rivalry between the United States and the USSR was played out at the Olympic Games. Both countries took great pride in defeating the other. The Soviet Union and its Eastern Bloc allies made success in the Olympic Games a very high priority. These countries believed that winning more Olympic medals than Western countries would prove that the Communist system was the best in the world.

Throughout the early decades of the Cold War, political problems between the United States and USSR did not affect Olympic competition. But the Soviet invasion of Afghanistan in 1979 changed this. Early in 1980, President Carter called for a boycott of the 1980 Summer Olympic Games, which were to be held in Moscow. Several Western nations, including the United States, Canada, and West Germany did not send athletes to the Games.

Soviet leaders were angered by the boycott. In 1984 they responded by boycotting the 1984 Summer Olympic Games, which were held in Los Angeles, California.

President Carter ordered the CIA to covertly (secretly) supply the anti-Soviet mujahideen with weapons and other military equipment. The Muslim fighters engaged in guerrilla warfare, causing heavy losses for the Soviets. By the end of 1980, 125,000 Soviet troops were stationed in Afghanistan. But the Soviets were unable to defeat the mujahideen. To make matters worse for the Soviets, Communism's anti-religious policies turned the Afghan war into a religious war. Thousands of Muslim men from the Middle East and other regions traveled to Afghanistan to fight "for Islam" against the Soviets. The situation was becoming as dangerous for the Soviets as Vietnam had been for the United States.

STRIKES IN POLAND

Meanwhile, the Soviet leadership began to experience problems in Poland. During the summer of 1980, Polish workers went on strike throughout the country to protest a sudden jump in the price of meat. (Poland's Communist government controlled these prices.) The massive wave of strikes closed factories and businesses, shutting down much of the country. Government officials negotiated an end to the strike, but it had united many Poles against the Communist government. The strikers formed a union, naming it Solidarnosc, or Solidarity (unity).

Polish Communist officials were alarmed by Solidarity. Unions were illegal in Communist states. A large, popular union could challenge the Communist Party's power. Warsaw Pact forces prepared for an invasion of Poland.

Throughout 1981 Solidarity continued to grow. By the end of the year, the union had 10 million members. Meanwhile, the country's economy continued to suffer. The Polish standard of living grew worse, and food shortages swept the country. Solidarity's leader, Lech Walesa, challenged the Polish government's policies.

Lech Walesa

Polish Communist leaders were in a tough position. Solidarity was challenging their power. But giving in to Solidarity would lead to a Warsaw Pact invasion. An invasion might then cause a war between Warsaw Pact forces and Polish citizens. On December 13, 1981, Polish prime minister General Wojciech Jaruzelski declared martial law. This brought out Polish troops and tanks on city streets to keep the peace. Walesa and thousands of other Solidarity leaders were arrested. Solidarity was banned.

A CHANGE IN U.S. POLICY

American leaders condemned Jaruzelski's actions. The new U.S. president, Ronald Reagan, promised a tough new approach to the Soviet Union. Reagan described the Soviet Union as an "evil empire." He criticized détente, saying it only encouraged undemocratic Soviet practices.

Since the beginning of the Cold War, the U.S. approach to the Soviets had been based on containing Communism. Few U.S. leaders ever discussed defeating the Soviet Union or actually winning the Cold War.

Reagan and his advisers saw things differently. They believed the troubles in Poland and Afghanistan showed that the Soviet Union was weakening. Reagan predicted the Communist system would someday end up on the "ash heap of history." Soviet leaders were alarmed by this tough talk. The thaw in the Cold War had come to an end.

9 REAGAN AND GORBACHEV

By the early 1980s, the Soviet economy was in deep trouble. For decades, the nation had spent about half of its national budget on defense and the military. The Soviets also gave billions of dollars to their allies. At the same time, the Soviets were also spending huge amounts of money fighting in Afghanistan.

To make matters worse, the Communist economic system was very inefficient. Workers earned low wages, so they had little reason to work hard. And so much of the nation's industry mostly made military equipment that not enough consumer goods were manufactured.

The Communist Party itself was also very inefficient. Party leaders, or "bosses," ran most industries. Many were corrupt and were interested only in holding on to their jobs. They were unwilling to make changes so that the country could keep up with the rest of the world. As a result, the Soviet Union and its allies began to fall behind. As the West began a computer revolution and updated its consumer and military industries, the Communist states continued on as before.

Reagan and his advisers targeted this weakness. They set out to cripple the Soviet Union. The United States began a new arms race. Reagan called for big increases in military spending. Congress approved new weapons programs, such as the supersonic B-1 bomber. The goal was to race until the Soviet Union was forced to give up.

Reagan's biggest blow was the announcement of plans for a Strategic Defense Initiative (SDI) in 1983. SDI was a space age defense system that would protect the United States from ICBM attack. Known as "Star Wars," SDI would create a missile shield of laser beams to shoot down attacking ICBMs. American scientists set to work to develop the system. Soviet leaders were forced to devote precious resources to developing their own SDI system.

Reagan also challenged the Soviets in other ways. He increased covert aid to the Afghan mujahideen. The United States also covertly supported other movements that challenged Communism in Eastern Europe, Central America, and Africa. As a result, the Soviets had to spend money to crush these movements.

Some Soviet leaders thought Reagan was crazy. So did some Americans. Many worried that Reagan might frighten the Soviets into attacking the United States.

They reasoned that if the Soviets felt overpowered, they might strike first. A surprise attack might be the only way for the Soviets to survive a nuclear war.

CHANGES IN LEADERSHIP

As the Soviet economy tottered, Soviet leaders changed often. Leonid Brezhnev had been ill for several years. His illness had left him unable to perform his duties. This lack of clear leadership added to the Soviet Union's many problems. Brezhnev died in November 1982.

Yuri Andropov, head of the KGB, replaced Brezhnev. But he died after a little more than a year in office. Andropov was replaced by Konstantin Chernenko. Yet Chernenko was also old and sick. He died after only a year in office. Without strong leadership, the Soviet Union continued to struggle during these years.

Finally, the Soviet Communist Party chose a younger man for the top post. On March 15, 1985, the day after Chernenko's death, the Communist Party chose a new leader, Mikhail Gorbachev.

Mikhail Gorbachev (center, behind Konstantin Chernenko's coffin) was chosen as the new leader of the Soviet Union in 1985. Communist officials hoped Gorbachev's youth and energy would help the Soviet Union rebound from its troubles.

Mikhail Gorbachev

Mikhail Sergeyevich Gorbachev was born into a peasant family on March 2, 1931, in the village of Privolnoye in southern Russia. A bright student, he studied law at Moscow State University. After graduating in 1955, Gorbachev returned to southern Russia to work for the Communist Party. His intelligence and energy won him many allies in the party. By 1980 Gorbachev had become a member of the Politburo, the Soviet Union's most powerful group of leaders. He took charge of the country's economy.

Gorbachev became famous before he took the top Soviet job in 1985. He had met with Western leaders to improve relations between the Soviet Union and the West. British prime minister Margaret Thatcher said of him, "I like Mr. Gorbachev. We can do business together."

GORBACHEV, PERESTROIKA, AND GLASNOST

Mikhail Gorbachev inherited many difficulties. But he had great energy and a sense of optimism about his country's future. He called for "new thinking" to create solutions to the Soviet Union's problems.

Gorbachev proposed two major changes. The first, *perestroika,* or "restructuring," called for a more efficient Soviet economy. Factory managers were given more freedom to produce goods that citizens wanted and needed. Private citizens were also allowed to start their own private businesses. Some farmers were given their own land. As a result, many farmers were more productive. For the first time, Western corporations were also encouraged to do business in the Soviet Union. For example, McDonald's restaurants soon opened in Moscow and in other Soviet cities.

Gorbachev's second major program was known as *glasnost,* or "openness." For the first time in the history of the Soviet Union, citizens and the media were allowed to openly criticize the government. Gorbachev hoped that this new openness would lead citizens to discuss the nation's problems. He believed these discussions would help the Soviet Union to find solutions.

Gorbachev realized that his country could no longer afford to support Communist regimes and revolutions in other nations. He also knew that many of his country's problems were due to its huge defense budget. The Soviet Union simply could not afford to spend so much money on its military. He was eager to resume détente and arms reductions. Gorbachev and Reagan agreed to meet to discuss these issues.

The appearance of Western businesses in the Soviet Union was one of the first visible signs of perestroika.

LIFE IN THE SOVIET UNION

The Communist revolution of 1917 had promised a "worker's paradise." All citizens would be equal and everyone would have the basic needs of life. According to the writings of Karl Marx, once a true Communist state was established, society would run perfectly by itself—no government would be necessary. Yet Marx's ideas were only theories. They had never been tested in real life. They never became reality.

While the Soviet Communist government did provide many citizens' most basic needs, such as housing, employment, education, and health care, it provided little else. For example, two luxuries that most Americans take for granted—televisions and automobiles—were rare and precious items in the USSR.

Housing was a constant problem in the Soviet Union. Although rent was cheap, most ordinary citizens lived in cramped "communal apartments," in which entire families lived within a single small room, sharing a kitchen, bathroom, and living room with other families. Citizens had little or no privacy. Communal living had been designed to strengthen citizens' bond with their community, but instead, it often created bitterness toward one's neighbors.

A woman works in the tiny kitchen of her eight-family apartment in Ashkhabad, Turkmenistan. Her cramped kitchen has no refrigerator.

The Communist system strongly discouraged religious practice. The Soviet government closed most churches, and worshipers were often forced to practice their faith at home, often in secret. Citizens who clung to their traditional religious beliefs risked harassment or even imprisonment by Communist leaders.

Communist leaders strictly controlled art in the Soviet Union. Artists were only allowed to create works that glorified Communism. Any artist who dared to criticize the government risked losing his or her job and could face imprisonment. Yet some risked punishment by secretly creating and passing around their works to citizens eager for new and exciting material.

By the early 1980s, a large percentage of Soviet citizens were fed up with the Communist system. Gorbachev unknowingly unleashed this anger by allowing more freedom in Soviet society. Perestroika gave Soviets a glimpse of capitalism. Citizens responded by demanding more goods and economic freedom. Glasnost allowed Soviet citizens to openly share their opinions about their government. The people responded with a flood of criticism, which ultimately led to the collapse of the Communist system.

SUMMIT MEETINGS

The two leaders held a series of summits to negotiate arms reductions. In November 1985, they met in Geneva, where the two leaders set some goals. These goals included cutting both nations' nuclear arsenals in half. In a joint statement, both leaders declared that "a nuclear war cannot be won and must not be fought."

A year later, Reagan and Gorbachev met again, this time in Reykjavik, on the island of Iceland in the North Atlantic Ocean. By this time, Gorbachev was desperate to make some major arms reductions. The Soviet economy remained weak. Gorbachev needed to cut spending on weapons. The Soviet leader offered huge cuts in nuclear weapons. Reagan offered even deeper cuts. He suggested eliminating all of the two countries' nuclear weapons within a decade.

The end of the superpower standoff was in sight. But Gorbachev insisted the deal include getting rid of SDI. Reagan refused. The president believed SDI was the key to safety from missile attacks. Yet both sides wanted to reduce their missile stockpiles. Whatever the case, the talks ended without an agreement. Both sides were disappointed with the result. But both leaders were also encouraged by the progress they had made. Nuclear disarmament seemed to be within reach.

THE CHERNOBYL ACCIDENT

Meanwhile, the Soviet Union continued to struggle economically. A terrible accident in the Soviet Republic of the Ukraine made

Reagan *(left)* and Gorbachev *(right)* parted ways in Reykjavik in 1986 without coming to an agreement on cutting nuclear weapons. But the talks had shown that the two leaders were making progress.

At first, the Soviet government wasn't sure what to do. So they did nothing. Most Soviet citizens learned about the explosion from Western radio broadcasts. As Soviets began asking questions, the government finally had to admit a disaster had occurred. Workers were sent in to try to clean up the mess. But these people quickly became ill from radiation sickness. Many of them died.

Finally, one week after the explosion, the Soviet government called for an evacuation (clearing) of the area. More than 135,000 people were forced to leave their homes. These people continue to suffer health problems, such as cancer and birth defects, due to their exposure to radiation.

A team of scientists tests for radiation over the demolished nuclear reactor at Chernobyl. Unsure how to clean up the mess, Soviet authorities simply buried the reactor under a massive pile of concrete.

matters far worse. On April 26, 1986, one of the reactors at the Chernobyl nuclear power plant exploded. Thirty-one people died in the explosion. Hundreds more were hospitalized. High levels of radiation poisoned the area around the accident. The huge blast sprayed radioactive fallout hundreds of miles across the western Soviet Union and into Europe.

A Major Embarrassment

On May 28, 1987, the Soviet Union's military was embarrassed by a daring nineteen-year-old German named Mathias Rust. Rust flew his small airplane from Helsinki through the heart of Russia, where he landed in Red Square, in the center of Moscow. Somehow, the young German's plane had slipped through the Soviet Union's air defense system, which was supposed to detect unidentified aircraft. Soviet police immediately arrested Rust.

The event made many people question how well the Soviet Union's military worked. Several top military officials were fired. Meanwhile, Rust was sentenced to eight years in prison for his stunt. But in August of 1988, Soviet officials released him as a show of friendship to the West.

The Chernobyl tragedy led to bitter resentment against the Soviet government. Citizens believed that the government had little regard for its people's welfare. Chernobyl and economic hardship made Gorbachev more and more unpopular at home. But people outside of the Soviet Union loved him. In the United States, glasnost and perestroika became household words. Gorbachev was praised for wanting to end the nuclear arms race once and for all. In December 1987, Reagan and Gorbachev signed the Intermediate Range Nuclear Forces (INF) Treaty in Washington, D.C. This treaty called for the elimination of medium-range nuclear missiles. This was a major step toward ending the nuclear arms race.

On May 14, 1988, the Soviet government signed an agreement to begin withdrawing troops from Afghanistan. By early 1989, all Soviet troops had left the country.

More changes came quickly. A few months before the last troops left Afghanistan, Gorbachev made a speech at the United Nations. He spoke of the importance of "freedom of choice." He announced that the Soviet Union would no longer try to control the governments of other nations. These countries would be able to choose their own paths without Soviet interference.

Gorbachev also made another stunning announcement. He declared that the Soviet Union would cut 500,000 men from its army. He also stated that 50,000 Soviet troops and 5,000 Soviet tanks would be removed from Eastern Bloc countries. Gorbachev was changing Cold War policies at breakneck speed. But at the time, few could have guessed what the next year would bring.

DEMOCRATIZATSIA

Gorbachev was allowing the Soviet people greater freedom. But the freedom of glasnost and perestroika made many Communist Party bosses uneasy. They felt the new policies were a threat to the Communist system and the Communist Party. Some of the bosses called for an end to the reforms and threatened to push Gorbachev out of power.

Gorbachev responded to the Communist bosses' threats in a spectacular way. He called for *democratizatsia*, or "democracy," in the Soviet Union. Gorbachev wanted elections. He believed people would choose his reforms over the old way of doing things.

In March 1989, the Soviet Union held its first free elections. More than 170 million citizens voted for candidates for the new Soviet legislature (lawmaking body), the Congress of People's Deputies. Many Communist Party leaders were voted out of office. The elections brought people in favor of reform to power.

Soon republics across the Soviet Union were calling for more freedom—even independence. In the Baltic states of Estonia, Latvia, and Lithuania, citizens and leaders declared their right to self-rule. Mass demonstrations in cities in Kazakhstan, Uzbekistan, and other Soviet Central Asian states also called for independence. Gorbachev had wanted change. But he wanted the Soviet Union to stay united. Yet his reforms had created a force for freedom beyond his control.

THE EASTERN BLOC CRUMBLES

Meanwhile, the fire of revolution was spreading across Eastern Europe. In

Poland the government legalized Solidarity in April 1989. Two months later, free elections were held. Solidarity candidates won a large number of seats in the Polish legislature. A Solidarity leader was chosen as prime minister. Poland had formed a non-Communist government.

In Hungary similar changes were taking place. In March 1989, the government allowed mass demonstrations against the government. In October new political parties were allowed to form. These new parties defeated the Communist Party in elections the following spring. Hungary became a democracy.

Anti-Communist demonstrations swept across East Germany in 1989. East German leader Erich Honecker resigned in October. As the East German government crumbled, tens of thousands of East Germans left the country. They crossed through Czechoslavakia and Hungary and into Austria. These first movements started a huge wave of people fleeing East Germany. Germany's leaders did not try to stop them. Border gates around the

The Tiananmen Square Massacre

In May 1989, millions of Chinese took to the streets to demand more freedom and democracy from their government. The largest protests took place in China's capital, Beijing. There, about one million citizens—mostly young students and workers—gathered peacefully to call for government reforms. In Tiananmen Square in the center of Beijing, protesters built a monument that looked like the U.S. Statue of Liberty. The protesters called the statue the Goddess of Democracy.

At first, Chinese leaders were not sure how to react to the popular movement. Some Communist leaders wanted to make changes, in hopes of satisfying the protesters. Others wanted to take a hard line—to crush the protesters with military force. Eventually, the hard-liners made the decision to destroy the democracy movement. On June 3, Chinese army tanks rolled into the streets of Beijing. Hundreds of unarmed protesters were killed. Thousands more were imprisoned. The entire massacre was covered on international television. Western nations strongly criticized China's actions. But the use of force kept the Communist Party in power in China.

A lone pro-democracy demonstrator stands in the path of Chinese Red Army tanks in Tiananmen Square. Many of the killed and wounded protesters were quickly taken away by Chinese officials. The exact number of people who died in the massacre is still unknown.

country, including the gates of the Berlin Wall, were opened. Berliners almost immediately began destroying the wall. In March 1990, free elections were held in East Germany. A non-Communist government came to power. In October, 45 years after the end of World War II, East and West Germany reunited as one nation.

At about the same time, tens of thousands of Czech citizens protested against their Communist government. In response, the Communists allowed some non-Communists into the government, but this was not enough to satisfy the public. Soon hundreds of thousands of Czechs were demonstrating against the Communist regime. Millions

> ### EYEWITNESS QUOTE: THE FALL OF THE BERLIN WALL
>
> **"Over 20,000 East and West Germans were gathered there in a huge party. . . . Between lanes of cars, streams of people were walking, talking together. Under one light, a group of musicians were playing violins and accordions and men and women were dancing."**
>
> —Andreas Ramos, Berliner

went on strike. Factories and businesses were shut down, crippling the country. Communist leader Gustav Husak resigned. In June of the following year, free elections were held in Czechoslovakia. Similar revolutions occurred in Bulgaria and Romania.

The Eastern Bloc was coming apart at the seams. But for the first time, Soviet troops weren't trying to stop the revolutions. Overjoyed observers declared 1989 the "year of the people" in Eastern Europe.

A SPECTACULAR BREAKUP

As the Eastern Bloc fell apart, the Soviet Union was also coming to an end. Since its beginning, the Soviet Union had been dominated by Russia and by the leaders in

Joyous Berliners celebrate the opening of the Berlin Wall in 1989. Within months, East and West Germany would be reunited.

Moscow. The non-Russian republics had resented this control. Early in 1990, Estonia, Latvia, and Lithuania all declared independence from the Soviet Union. By the end of the year, other Soviet republics had begun calling for independence. These changes went far beyond what Gorbachev had wanted. To try to slow things down, he offered the Soviet republics a compromise. In July 1991, he called for a new, looser union. This new federation would give the non-Russian republics more control over their own affairs than they had had in the past.

New U.S. president George H. W. Bush looked on in amazement. He and other U.S. leaders were not sure what to do. Said one U.S. official, "It [the fall of Communism in Eastern Europe and the Soviet Union] is going much faster than anyone might have anticipated." U.S. leaders feared a sudden, violent reaction from the Communist bosses. Would they try to recapture power by force?

These fears came to life when a group of hard-line Communists attempted a coup on August 19, 1991. The coup leaders placed Gorbachev under arrest and hoped that Soviet citizens would support their move. But the coup failed to gain support from Soviet citizens. Although Gorbachev was unpopular, citizens did not want to see a return to the old Communist way. Thousands of Soviet citizens appeared on the streets to protest the coup. The president of Russia, Boris Yeltsin, was their leader. Still, the coup plotters hoped to get the army to support them, in hopes that troops would crush the demonstrations. But the Soviet army refused to act against the demonstrators. By August 21, the coup attempt had collapsed.

NICOLAE CEAUSESCU

Only one Communist dictator, Nicolae Ceausescu of Romania, lost his life during the fall of the Eastern Bloc. Convicted of crimes against the Romanian people for their harsh rule, Ceausescu and his wife were executed on December 25, 1989.

FAST FACT

Gorbachev returned to power. But he remained deeply unpopular. His reforms had not worked. The Soviet economy remained weak. A typical Russian earned one-tenth as much as a typical American each year. Consumer goods remained scarce. Inflation skyrocketed. The few goods available were often too expensive for citizens to buy.

In December Russia, Belarus, and the Ukraine declared their independence from the Soviet Union. They formed a Commonwealth of Independent States

Nuclear Weapons after the Cold War

The collapse of the Soviet Union may have ended the threat of a worldwide nuclear war, but the fear of nuclear weapons remains. U.S. and UN officials are especially concerned about nuclear weapons ending up in the hands of terrorists. The Soviet Union held thousands of nuclear weapons at the time of its breakup. Officials in the United States and at the UN have expressed fears that former Soviet weapons under the control of the former Soviet republics could be illegally sold to terrorist groups.

(CIS). Within a few weeks, eleven other Soviet republics joined the CIS. Suddenly, Gorbachev was a leader without a country. On December 25, 1991, he resigned from his post. On that day, the Soviet Union ceased to exist. The Cold War was over.

A group of young Russians stands next to a fallen statue of Stalin in Moscow. Many statues of former Soviet leaders were pulled down in celebrations marking the end of the Cold War.

THE END OF THE COLD WAR

Throughout most of the Cold War years, the world lived in fear of a nuclear war that might kill hundreds of millions of people and possibly destroy all life on earth. Yet the collapse of the Soviet Union and the breakup of the Eastern Bloc happened with almost no loss of life. No major wars or battles were fought to end Communist rule in Europe and the Soviet Union.

The effects of the Cold War continue. The economies of the former Soviet republics and the Eastern Bloc countries are still recovering from decades of Communist rule. The Communist parties in these countries had controlled the economy for so long that changing over to a capitalist system has been very difficult. Few citizens in these countries have had the money or the experience needed to start and run private businesses.

For example, the former East Germany had had the strongest economy of the Eastern Bloc countries. Yet more than 10 years after reunification with West Germany, the states that make up the former East Germany still have economic problems, such as few jobs and low wages. Since reunification, millions of residents of the former East Germany have moved to the former West Germany in search of jobs and better wages.

The countries that once made up the Soviet Union also continue to struggle. In Russia severe economic problems followed the breakup of the Soviet Union. High inflation (rising prices combined with a drop in the value of Russian money) crippled the country's economy. Everyday items such as shoes, toilet paper, and clothes became unaffordable for many Russians. Food and

Poverty, alcoholism, and homelessness remain serious problems throughout the former Soviet republics.

shelter, which had once been provided by the state, also became too expensive for some citizens. As a result, many Russians were left homeless and hungry. Other former Soviet republics have had similar problems.

COMMUNISM AFTER THE COLD WAR

In the 2000s, Communist governments rule only four countries—China, North Korea, Cuba, and Vietnam. These countries remain undemocratic, and their economies have struggled under Communism. Since the end of the Cold War, China and Vietnam have made reforms to their economies. They have allowed more private businesses to be cre-

ated and allowed more Western goods to be sold in their countries. As a result, these countries have enjoyed improved standards of living. But citizens in these countries are still not allowed to criticize their governments without fear of imprisonment. Both countries have jailed thousands of dissidents over the years.

Fidel Castro continues to rule Cuba. While Cubans receive free health care and education, the country remains very poor. Dissent is still not allowed under Castro's regime. In May 2003, 75 Cubans were sentenced to long prison terms for calling for democracy in Cuba. The U.S. embargo on Cuba continues, adding to the country's low standard of living.

Some Americans think the embargo should be lifted because it is harming only the Cuban people, not Castro. They hope that ending it would also create a more open society by allowing more American travelers and businesspeople to visit Cuba. Others feel that lifting the embargo would only reward Castro's unlawful rule.

North Korea is ruled by the totalitarian dictator Kim Jong Il, the son of Kim Il Sung. Most of the country's citizens are poor, and more than one million North Koreans died of hunger in the late 1990s. The country relies on aid from its neighbors for food, fuel, and other needs.

Despite its economic problems, North Korea continues to spend billions on its military and on weapons. Although it signed the Nuclear Non-Proliferation Treaty decades earlier, the North Korean government said in 2002 that it was developing nuclear weapons. Kim Jong Il's regime said the weapons were being built to deter attacks from hostile nations, in particular, the United States. In 2002 U.S. president George W. Bush accused North Korea of selling weapons to terrorists and to nations that supported terrorism.

Some of the mujahideen who fought against the Soviet troops in Afghanistan have come to see the United States—the world's only superpower—as Islam's greatest enemy. They believe that the United States is trying to destroy Islam and control the heartland of Islam, the oil-rich Middle East. Many of these fighters joined the international terrorist organization al-Qaeda. Al-Qaeda's leader, Osama bin Laden, fought against the Soviets in Afghanistan. Al-Qaeda terrorists have been blamed for several terrorist attacks on U.S. targets, including the September 11, 2001, attacks on the World Trade Center towers in New York City and the Pentagon, the U.S. military headquarters in Alexandria, Virginia. U.S. forces invaded Afghanistan in October 2001 to destroy al-Qaeda bases and to

Late in 2002, North Korea revealed it was using the material from this nuclear power plant to build nuclear weapons. North Korean officials claimed the weapons were being built to deter a U.S. attack. U.S. officials fear North Korea will try to sell its weapons to terrorists or to nations hostile to the United States.

New York's World Trade Center towers, moments after the terrorist attacks of September 11, 2001. The attacks opened a new kind of war—the war on terrorism. The sense of relief some Americans felt at the end of the Cold War has been replaced by the fear of terrorist attacks.

destroy the Afghan government that protected them. U.S. officials worry that al-Qaeda or other terrorist groups are trying to build or purchase nuclear weapons to use against the United States.

THE COSTS OF THE COLD WAR

Although the Cold War never became a hot war, millions of people lost their lives in the fight between Communism and anti-Communism. Millions of soldiers and civilians died in wars in Korea, Vietnam, Afghanistan, and other countries around the world. Millions more were left homeless by war or were imprisoned because they spoke out against their governments. The Cold War's arms race saw the United States and the Soviet Union spending trillions of dollars on weapons and military expenses.

In 1992 President George H. W. Bush declared that the United States had "won the Cold War." Gorbachev viewed things differently. "I do not regard the end of the Cold War as a victory for one side," he said. "The end of the Cold War is our common victory." In a way, both leaders were correct. The United States came out of the Cold War as the most powerful nation on earth. Yet the fact that the Cold War ended without a nuclear war was a victory for the entire world.

SELECTED EVENTS OF THE COLD WAR

Yalta Conference of Allied leaders	February 1945
Potsdam Conference of Allied leaders	July–August 1945
Berlin Airlift	June 1948–May 1949
Korean War	1950–1953
Hungarian Revolution	October–November 1956
Bay of Pigs Invasion, Cuba	April 17, 1961
Cuban Missile Crisis	October 1962
The Vietnam War	1950s–1975
The Prague Spring, Czechoslovakia	January–August 1968
Signing of the Helsinki Accords, Helsinki, Finland	July 31–August 1, 1975
Soviet war in Afghanistan	1979–1989
Reagan and Gorbachev summit in Reykjavik, Iceland	October 1986
The fall of the Berlin Wall	November 1989

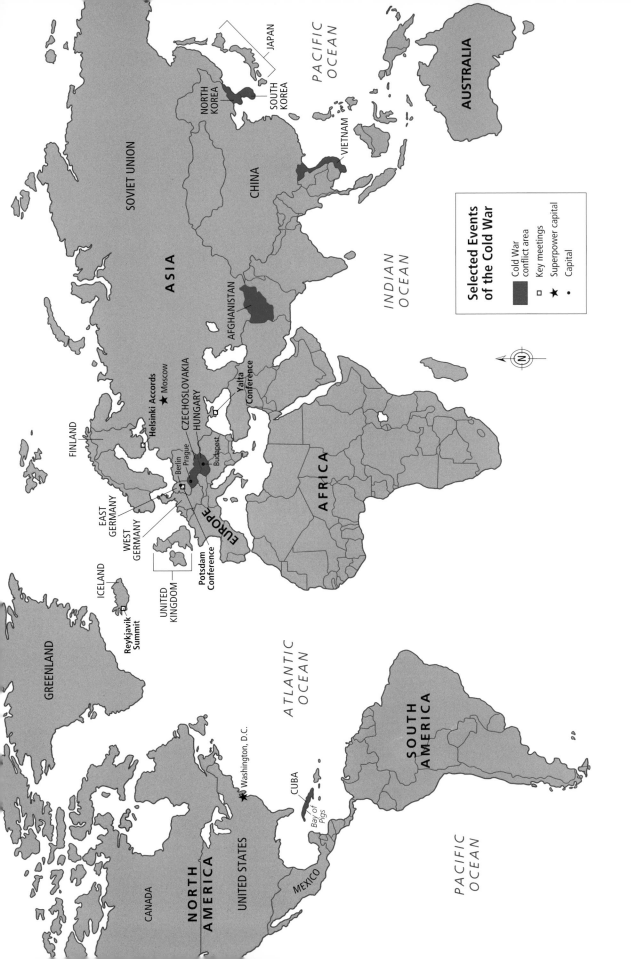

Selected Events of the Cold War

- Cold War conflict area
- □ Key meetings
- ★ Superpower capital
- • Capital

N

PACIFIC OCEAN

JAPAN

NORTH KOREA

SOUTH KOREA

VIETNAM

CHINA

SOVIET UNION

ASIA

AFGHANISTAN

AUSTRALIA

INDIAN OCEAN

Helsinki Accords
★ Moscow

CZECHOSLOVAKIA

HUNGARY

Yalta Conference

FINLAND

Berlin
Prague
Budapest

EAST GERMANY

WEST GERMANY

EUROPE

AFRICA

Potsdam Conference

ICELAND

UNITED KINGDOM

Reykjavik Summit

GREENLAND

NORTH AMERICA

CANADA

UNITED STATES

★ Washington, D.C.

MEXICO

CUBA

Bay of Pigs

ATLANTIC OCEAN

SOUTH AMERICA

PACIFIC OCEAN

COLD WAR TIMELINE

1922	V. I. Lenin's Communist Party forms the Union of Soviet Socialist Republics (USSR).
1939	World War II begins.
1945	The Yalta Conference of Allied leaders is held February 4–11.
	The Potsdam Conference is held from July 17–August 2.
	The United States drops two atomic bombs on Japan in August.
	Japan surrenders on September 2, ending World War II.
1947	U.S. secretary of state George C. Marshall proposes an aid program—the Marshall Plan—to rebuild Europe on June 5.
1948	USSR blocks land access to Berlin on June 24. Berlin Airlift begins.
1949	North Atlantic Treaty is signed on April 4.
	USSR lifts Berlin blockade on May 12.
	USSR tests its first atomic bomb on August 29.
1950	North Korea invades South Korea, sparking the Korean War (1950-1953).
1955	The Eastern Bloc and USSR form the Warsaw Pact on May 14.
1956	Soviet forces crush an uprising against Communist rule in Hungary, October–November.
1962	In October U.S. officials discover Soviet nuclear missiles in Cuba, sparking the Cuban Missile Crisis.
1968	Czech citizens call for more freedom, giving rise to the Prague Spring.
	The United States, USSR, and Great Britain sign the Nuclear Non-Proliferation Treaty on July 1.
	Warsaw Pact troops invade Czechoslovakia to crush the Prague Spring on August 20–21.
1972	The United States and USSR sign the SALT Treaty on May 26.
1973	A peace agreement is signed on January 27, ending U.S. involvement in the Vietnam War.
1975	Thirty-five countries sign the Helsinki Accords on July 30–August 1.
1979	Soviet forces invade Afghanistan in December.
1983	President Reagan announces Strategic Defense Initiative on March 23.
1985	Soviet premier Gorbachev announces glasnost and perestroika.
1986	President Reagan and Gorbachev meet to discuss nuclear arms reduction.
1989	Soviet troops withdraw from Afghanistan.
	USSR holds its first free elections on March 26.
	Democracy movements sweep across the Eastern Bloc.
	The Berlin Wall is opened on November 9.
1991	USSR is dissolved, ending the Cold War, on December 25.

GLOSSARY

arsenal: supply of weapons

atomic bomb: a powerful nuclear bomb, capable of destroying an entire city

blacklist: a list of persons who are disapproved of or are targeted for boycott or punishment; to place someone on a blacklist

blockade: an action that closes an area, such as a city, from being reached from the outside

capitalism: an economic system in which most property, goods, and businesses are privately owned, and most trade is based on supply and demand

Communism: a system in which the government owns most property and controls most labor and trade

democracy: a form of government in which people elect their leaders and representatives

détente: a French word referring to the relaxing or loosening of something strained. Détente was used to describe improvement of relations between the Soviet Union and the United States in the 1970s.

dissent: to criticize or differ in opinion, often in relation to one's government

fallout: radioactive particles left over from a nuclear explosion

glasnost: a Russian word meaning "openness." Glasnost described the policy of openness in public discussions encouraged by Soviet leader Gorbachev in the Soviet Union in the 1980s.

Iron Curtain: a term coined by British prime minister Winston Churchill for the Communist barrier countries between the West and the Soviet Union

martial law: a period when the military takes over law enforcement duties from the civilian police in order to keep the peace

nuclear winter: a term used to describe what might happen to the earth after a worldwide nuclear war. In nuclear winter scenarios, the sun would be blocked out by a dust cloud, and radioactive fallout would spread across the earth

perestroika: a Russian word meaning "restructuring." Perestroika was the term used to describe Soviet leader Gorbachev's policy of restructuring the Soviet economy.

summit: a meeting of high-level leaders

totalitarianism: a system of government under which the public and the economy are strictly controlled by the state, often by means of force

WHO'S WHO?

George Herbert Walker Bush (b. 1924)

George Herbert Walker Bush, forty-first president of the United States, was born in Milton, Massachusetts. After serving as a pilot in the U.S. Navy during World War II, Bush went to Yale University. In 1966 Bush won a seat in the U.S. House of Representatives. After holding many important government positions in the 1970s, he was elected to the vice presidency in Ronald Reagan's successful 1980 presidential campaign. Bush was elected president in 1988, as the Soviet Union and the Eastern Bloc were beginning to collapse.

Fidel Castro (b. 1926)

Fidel Castro was born Fidel Casto Ruz in Birán, Cuba. The son of a plantation owner, Castro studied law at the University of Havana in the late 1940s. In 1952 he ran for political office in Cuba, but Cuban dictator Fulgencio Batista canceled the elections. As a result, Castro led a revolution against Batista's government. After years of guerrilla attacks by Castro's forces, Batista fled and Castro declared himself ruler of Cuba, turning the country into a Communist state. Castro has lent support—in the form of soldiers, arms, and money—to Communist revolutions in many countries, including Angola, Nicaragua, and Bolivia.

Sir Winston Churchill (1874–1965)

As prime minister of Great Britain, Churchill led his country to victory during World War II. Born in Oxfordshire, England, to a wealthy noble family, Churchill joined the British Royal Army, where he served as a soldier and a journalist. He was first voted into public office in 1900. He served in many important posts in the following decades, and in 1940 became prime minister. Following World War II, Churchill called for tough tactics against Soviet expansion in Eastern Europe, coining the phrase the "Iron Curtain" in a 1946 speech.

Ho Chi Minh (1890–1969)

Born in central Vietnam, Ho spent much of his youth traveling the world. In 1941 he returned to Vietnam to form the Viet Minh, a group that fought for Vietnamese independence. Ho Chi Minh first battled the French and later the United States to unite Vietnam under Communist rule. Ho died of a heart attack six years before the end of the Vietnam War.

J. Edgar Hoover (1895–1972)

John Edgar Hoover served as director of the FBI for 48 years, from 1924 until his death. Born in Washington, D.C., he attended George Washington University. After graduating with a law degree, Hoover joined the United States Department of Justice. As FBI director, Hoover led a long campaign against Communists in the United States, often violating the Constitution in order to spy on and harass suspected Communists.

Mao Zedong (1893–1976)

Born in Hunan Province, in southeast central China, to a peasant farmer family, Mao was a founding member of the Chinese Communist Party. After a long and bloody civil war, Mao founded the People's Republic of China on October 1, 1949. As ruler of China, Mao isolated his country from the West for more than two decades. In the 1960s, Mao led the Cultural Revolution, a movement to destroy capitalism, anti-Communism, and traditional Chinese culture in China. About 100 million Chinese were executed or imprisoned during this period.

Joseph McCarthy (1908–1957)

Born in Grand Chute, Wisconsin, Joseph McCarthy was elected to the U.S. Senate in 1946. He served during the height of the Red Scare of the late-1940s and early 1950s. As a member of the House Un-American Activities Committee, McCarthy used rough tactics and unfair accusations to hound suspected Communists and to gain attention for himself. His method of bullying witnesses and falsely accusing people came to be known as "McCarthyism."

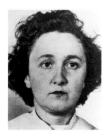

Ethel Rosenberg (1915–1953)

Born to a poor family in New York City, Ethel Rosenberg joined the American Communist Party in the 1930s. She married Julius Rosenberg in 1939 and bore two sons. In 1950 Julius was arrested on charges of espionage, and soon Ethel was also accused of spying for the government. Ethel's younger brother, David Greenglass, also a convicted spy, accused the couple of being part of a Communist spy ring. Ethel and Julius were convicted of espionage by the U.S. government and put to death in the electric chair in 1953.

Valentina Vladimirovna Tereshkova (b. 1937)

Soviet cosmonaut Valentina Tereshkova was the first woman to travel in space. Born near Yaroslavl in central Russia, she worked in a textile mill as a young woman. After developing an interest in parachuting, she won a spot in the Soviet cosmonaut training program. On June 16, 1963, she accomplished her historic space mission, making 45 orbits around the earth in a 70-hour, 50-minute flight.

Margaret Thatcher (b. 1925)

Thatcher served from 1979 to 1990 as the first woman prime minister of Great Britain. Born in Grantham, Lincolnshire, England, she was elected to Great Britain's House of Commons in 1959 and served as secretary of education and science in the early 1970s. As prime minister of Great Britain, she supported President Reagan's tough approach to the Soviet Union in the 1980s.

SOURCE NOTES

6 Gwladys Fouché, "The Cuban Missile Crisis," *Guardian Unlimited,* October 14, 2002, <http://www.guardian.co.uk/cuba/story/0,11983,811821,00.html> (June 6, 2003).

8 U.S. Constitution, amend. 1.

10 Tom Streissguth, *Life in Communist Russia* (San Diego, CA: Lucent Books, 2001), 10.

12 A. Mitchell Palmer, "The Case Against the 'Reds,'" *Center for History and New Media, George Mason University Website,* n.d., <http://chnm.gmu.edu/courses/hist409/palmer.html> (June 6, 2003).

18 David McCullough, *Truman* (New York: Simon and Schuster, 1992), 353.

20 "Marshall Plan Episode 3: Interview with Professor Theodore Geiger, February 17, 1996," *George Washington University Website,* n.d., <http://www.gwu.edu/~nsarchiv/coldwar/interviews/episode-3/geiger1.html> (June 4, 2003).

21 Terry O'Neill, ed, *The Nuclear Age* (San Diego, CA: Greenhaven Press, Inc., 2002), 39.

22 Jeremy Isaacs and Taylor Downing, *The Cold War: An Illustrated History, 1945–1991* (Boston: Little, Brown and Company, 1998), 34.

22 Harry S. Truman, "Student Activity: Harry Truman and the Truman Doctrine," *Truman Presidential Museum and Library,* n.d., <http://www.trumanlibrary.org/teacher/doctrine.htm> (June 4, 2003).

22 George C. Marshall, "The Marshall Plan: The Harvard Speech," *George C. Marshall Foundation,* 2002 <http://www.marshallfoundation.org/about_gcm/marshall_plan.htm#harvard_speech> (June 4, 2003).

23 Ronald Steel, "Playing Loose with History," *New York Times,* May 26, 1997. Reprinted on the Web at <http://www.mtholyoke.edu/acad/intrel/steel.htm> (June 19, 2003).

27 U.S. Constitution, amend. 4.

29 Griffin Fariello, *Red Scare: Memories of the American Inquisition* (New York: W. W. Norton and Company, 1995), 295.

29 Ellen Schrecker, *Many Are the Crimes: McCarthyism in America* (Boston: Little, Brown and Company, 1998), 327.

34 Ibid., 258.

34 Isaacs and Downing, *The Cold War,* 109.

35 Schrecker, *Many Are the Crimes,* 263.

35 Ibid., 264.

36 Ibid., 41.

36 Fariello, *Red Scare,* 226.

38 Isaacs and Downing, *The Cold War,* 87.

47 Howard Zinn, *The Twentieth Century: A People's History,* rev. ed. (New York: Harper Collins Publishers, Inc., 1998), 179.

49 Isaacs and Downing, *The Cold War,* 194.

49 Ibid., 200.

50 Ibid., 201.

51 "President John F. Kennedy on the Nuclear Test Ban, July 26, 1963," *Comprehensive Test Ban Treaty Site,* n.d., <http://www.clw.org/pub/clw/coalition/ken0763.htm> (May 27, 2003).

52 Norman Friedman, *The Fifty-Year War: Conflict and Strategy in the Cold War* (Annapolis, MD: Naval Institute Press, 2000), 234.

53 John F. Kennedy, "Special Message to the Congress on Urgent National Needs, May 25, 1961," *John F. Kennedy Library and Museum,* October 27, 2002, <http://www.cs.umb.edu/jfklibrary/j052561.htm> (June 4, 2003).

57 Allan M. Winkler, *The Cold War: A History in Documents* (New York: Oxford University Press, 2000), 121.

60 Schrecker, *Many Are the Crimes,* 32.

61 Isaac J. Tarasulo, ed., *Perils of Perestroika: Viewpoints from the Soviet Press, 1989–1991* (Wilmington, DE: SR Books, 1992), 25.

67 "Conference on Security and Cooperation in Europe. Final Act, Helsinki, 1 August 1975," *Hellenic Resources Network,* September 26, 1995. <http://www.hri.org/docs/Helsinki75.html#H4.7> (May 29, 2003).

67 Isaacs and Downing, *The Cold War,* 289.

68 Ibid., 312.

68 Michael Kort, *The Columbia Guide to the Cold War* (New York: Columbia University Press, 1998), 73.

69 Isaacs and Downing, *The Cold War,* 327.

71 Walter LaFeber, *America, Russia, and the Cold War, 1945–1992,* 7th ed. (New York: McGraw Hill, Inc, 1993), 304.

74 Ibid., 321.

74 Isaacs and Downing, *The Cold War,* 351.

76 Ibid., 363.

80 Andreas Ramos, " A Personal Account of the Fall of the Berlin Wall," *Andreas.com,* 1989, <http://www.andreas.com/berlin.html> (June 19, 2003).

81 LaFeber, *America, Russia, and the Cold War,* 335.

85 Isaacs and Downing, *The Cold War,* 418.

85 Ibid., 417.

SELECTED BIBLIOGRAPHY, FURTHER READING, & WEBSITES

SELECTED BIBLIOGRAPHY

Barson, Michael, and Stephen Heller. *Red Scared! The Commie Menace in Propaganda and Popular Culture.* San Francisco: Chronicle Books, 2001.

Friedman, Norman. *The Fifty-Year War: Conflict and Strategy in the Cold War.* Annapolis, MD: Naval Institute Press, 2000.

Isaacs, Jeremy, and Taylor Downing. *The Cold War: An Illustrated History, 1945–1991.* Boston: Little, Brown and Company, 1998.

Karnow, Stanley. *Vietnam: A History.* London and New York: Penguin Books, 1984.

Kotkin, Steven. *Armageddon Averted: The Soviet Collapse, 1970–2000.* London and New York: Oxford University Press, 2001.

MacDonald, Callum A. *Korea: The War before Vietnam.* New York: The Free Press, 1986.

Thomas, Hugh. *The Cuban Revolution.* New York: Harper & Row, 1977.

Walker, Martin. *The Cold War: A History.* New York: Henry Holt, 1995.

FURTHER READING

Behnke, Alison. *Afghanistan in Pictures.* Minneapolis: Lerner Publications Company, 2003.

———. *China in Pictures.* Minneapolis, MN: Lerner Publications Company, 2003.

Benson, Michael. *Ronald Reagan.* Minneapolis: Lerner Publications Company, 2004.

Farman, John. *The Short and Bloody History of Spies.* Minneapolis: Lerner Publications Company, 2002.

Feldman, Ruth Tenzer. *The Korean War.* Minneapolis: Lerner Publications Company, 2004.

Gherman, Beverly. *Jimmy Carter.* Minneapolis: Lerner Publications Company, 2004.

Lazo, Caroline. *Harry S. Truman.* Minneapolis: Lerner Publications Company, 2003.

Levy, Debbie. *Lyndon B. Johnson.* Minneapolis: Lerner Publications Company, 2003.

———. *The Vietnam War.* Minneapolis: Lerner Publications Company, 2004.

Márquez, Herón. *Richard M. Nixon.* Minneapolis: Lerner Publications Company, 2003.

———. *Russia in Pictures.* Minneapolis: Lerner Publications Company, 2004.

Taus-Bolstad, Stacy. *Czech Republic in Pictures.* Minneapolis: Lerner Publications Company, 2003.

———. *Vietnam in Pictures.* Minneapolis: Lerner Publications Company, 2003.

Zuehlke, Jeffrey. *Germany in Pictures.* Minneapolis: Lerner Publications Company, 2003.

WEBSITES

The American Experience: Vietnam Online. This website is the online companion to the award-winning PBS *American Experience* miniseries about the Vietnam War, *Vietnam: A Television History.* <http://www.pbs.org/wgbh/amex/vietnam>

CNN Interactive: Cold War. This website is a companion to CNN's award-winning 24-episode series, *Cold War.* <http://www.cnn.com/SPECIALS/cold.war/>

The Cold War Museum. Learn more about Cold War spies, weapons, and personalities at this online museum. <http://www.coldwar.org>

NATO Official Home Page. The official website of the North Atlantic Treaty Organization contains news and information about the alliance and its member nations. <http://www.nato.int/>

Newseum: Berlin Wall. This online museum features several fascinating exhibits about the Berlin Wall. <http://www.newseum.org/cybernewseum/exhibits/berlin_wall/index.htm>

Nova Online: Secrets, Lies, and Atomic Spies. A companion site to PBS's *Nova* program on spies, this website features information on the Venona documents, the Rosenbergs, and profiles of some of the Cold War's most famous secret agents. <http://www.pbs.org/wgbh/nova/verona/>

The United Nations Home Page. Go to the official UN website to learn more about the organization and the UN's many branches and bodies. <http://www.un.org/>

U.S. Air Forces in Europe Berlin Airlift Website. This U.S. Air Force website has lots of facts, figures, and photos about the Berlin Airlift. <http://www.usafe.af.mil/berlin/berlin.htm>

INDEX

ABOUT THE AUTHOR

Josepha Sherman is a fantasy novelist, freelance editor, and folklorist. She has also written for the educational market on everything from Bill Gates to the workings of the human ear. She is a fan of the New York Mets, horses, aviation, and space science. Visit her at <http://www.Josepha.Sherman.com>.

PHOTO ACKNOWLEDGMENTS

The images in this book are used with the permission of: © CORBIS, pp. 4–5, 48, 60; © Karl Weatherly/CORBIS, p. 6; Library of Congress, pp. 7, 11, 27, 31, 36, 91 (third from top); Independent Picture Service, p. 9; The Illustrated London News, pp. 10, 14, 90 (third from top), 91 (top); © Bettmann/CORBIS, pp. 12, 17, 23, 28, 33, 34, 40, 44, 45, 47, 62, 63, 67 (top), 90 (bottom); © Underwood & Underwood/CORBIS, p. 13; National Archives, pp. 15, 18, 19 (both), 20, 54, 55 (both), 65 (both), 90 (second from bottom); Fitzpatrick in the *St. Lous Post-Dispatch*, photo courtesy of State Historical Society of Missouri, Columbia, p. 16; Laura Westlund, pp. 21, 24 (both), 39, 56, 87; Harry S. Truman Library, p. 22; © Hulton-Deutsch Collection/CORBIS, pp. 25, 30, 37, 91 (second from bottom); U.S. Army, pp. 35, 91 (second from top); United Nations, p. 41; Hulton/Archive, pp. 42, 43, 69, 70, 72; Organization of American States, p. 46; Minnesota DFL Party, pp. 49, 57; John F. Kennedy Library, p. 50; NASA, pp. 52 (both), 53, 67 (bottom); United Press International Photo by Kyoichi Saudao, p. 58; © Miroslav Zajíc/CORBIS, p. 59; The Hoover Company, North Canton, Ohio, p. 61; © James A. Sugar/CORBIS, p. 64; The White House, p. 68; © Alain Nogues/CORBIS SYGMA, p. 73; © Liba Taylor/CORBIS, p. 74; © Shepard Sherbell/CORBIS, p. 75; Ronald Reagan Library, p. 76; © Kostin Igor/CORBIS SYGMA, p. 77; © Reuters NewMedia Inc./CORBIS, p. 79; German Information Center, p. 80; © Peter Turnley/CORBIS, p. 82; © Attal Serge/CORBIS SYGMA, p. 83; © AFP/CORBIS, p. 84; © Chris Collins/CORBIS, p. 85; George Bush for President, p. 90 (top); Archives and Special Collections Department, Otto G. Richter Library, University of Miami, Coral Gables, FL, p. 90 (second from top); © Richard Olivier/CORBIS, p. 91 (bottom).

Cover: © Steve Crise/CORBIS